GREATEST SPORTS MOMEN

SHOWDOWN IN MANILA

ALI AND FRAZIER'S EPIC FINAL FIGHT

BY MATT DOEDEN

ILLUSTRATED BY EDUARDO GARCIA AND RED WOLF STUDIO

CONSULTANT:
BRUCE BERGLUND
PROFESSOR OF HISTORY, CALVIN COLLEGE
GRAND RAPIDS, MICHIGAN

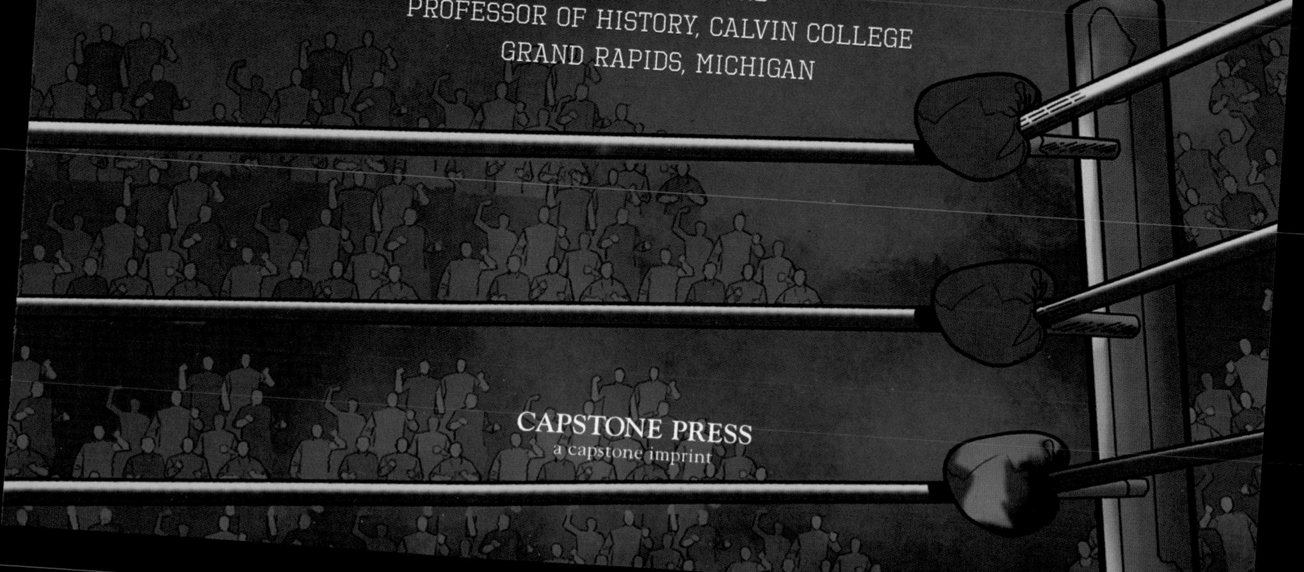

CAPSTONE PRESS
a capstone imprint

Graphic Library is published by Capstone Press,
1710 Roe Crest Drive, North Mankato, Minnesota 56003
www.mycapstone.com

Library of Congress Cataloging-in-Publication data
Names: Doeden, Matt, author. | Garcia, Eduardo, 1970, August 31–illustrator.
Title: Showdown in Manila: Ali and Frazier's epic final fight / by Matt Doeden ; Illustrated by Eduardo Garcia.
Description: North Mankato, Minnesota : Graphic Library, an imprint of Capstone Press, [2019] |
    Series: Graphic Library. Greatest Sports Moments | Includes index.
Identifiers: LCCN 2018001972 (print) | LCCN 2018010915 (ebook) | ISBN 9781543528749 (eBook PDF) |
    ISBN 9781543528664 (hardcover) | ISBN 9781543528701 (paperback)
Subjects: LCSH: Boxing matches—History. | Ali, Muhammad, 1942–2016. | Frazier, Joe, 1944–2011. |
    African American boxers–Biography. | Sports—History.
Classification: LCC GV1121 (ebook) | LCC GV1121 .D64 2018 (print) | DDC 796.8309599/16—dc23
LC record available at https://lccn.loc.gov/2018001972

Summary: Tells the story of the epic 1975 boxing match between Muhammad Ali and Joe Frazier that took place in Manila, Philippines.

EDITOR
Aaron J. Sautter

ART DIRECTOR
Nathan Gassman

DESIGNER
Ted Williams

MEDIA RESEARCHER
Eric Gohl

PRODUCTION SPECIALIST
Laura Manthe

Direct quotations appear in **bold italicized text** on the following pages:

Page 6: from "The Epic Battle," by SI Wire, Sports Illustrated, October 1, 2015 (https://www.si.com/boxing/2015/10/01/muhammad-ali-vs-joe-frazier-thrilla-manilla-video-anniversary).

Page 10: from "Thrilla in Manila: The Greatest Fight of All Time," by David Williams, GQ, October 1, 2015 (http://www.gq-magazine.co.uk/article/8-amazing-facts-about-muhammed-ali-thrilla-in-manilla).

Page 15: from "Jerry Izenberg in the Boxing Hall of Fame," by Mike Ricciardelli, The Queensbury Rules, December 30, 2015 (http://thecomeback.com/queensberryrules/2015-articles/jerry-izenberg-in-the-boxing-hall-of-fame.html).

Page 17: from Joe Frazier obituary, The Telegraph, November 8, 2011 (https://www.telegraph.co.uk/news/obituaries/sport-obituaries/8875960/Joe-Frazier.html).

Page 19: from "40 Years After 'Thrilla in Manila,' Under Armour Launching Muhammad Ali Collection," by Michael McCarthy, October 2, 2015 (http://www.sportingnews.com/other-sports/news/muhammad-ali-under-armour-joe-frazier-thrilla-in-manila-nick-woodhouse-abg-gleasons-gym/jwgx95qgz3jv19tudqixw2nxs).

Page 26, 27: from "Joe Frazier, R.I.P.," by David Remnick, The New Yorker, November 8, 2011 (https://www.newyorker.com/news/sporting-scene/joe-frazier-r-i-p).

Page 28, top: from Ghosts of Manila: The Fateful Blood Feud Between Muhammad Ali and Joe Frazier by Mark Kram. (New York: Harper Collins, 2002).

Page 28, middle: from "Why Muhammad Ali Matters to Everyone," by Sean Gregory, Time, June 4, 2016 (http://time.com/3646214/muhammad-ali-dead-obituary).

Page 28, bottom: from "Twenty-Five Years Later, Ali and Frazier Are Still Slugging It Out," by William Mack, Sports Illustrated, September 24, 2015 (www.si.com/boxing/2015/09/24/muhammad-ali-joe-frazier-william-nack-si-vault).

Printed and bound in the United States of America.
PA017

TABLE OF CONTENTS

A BITTER RIVALRY

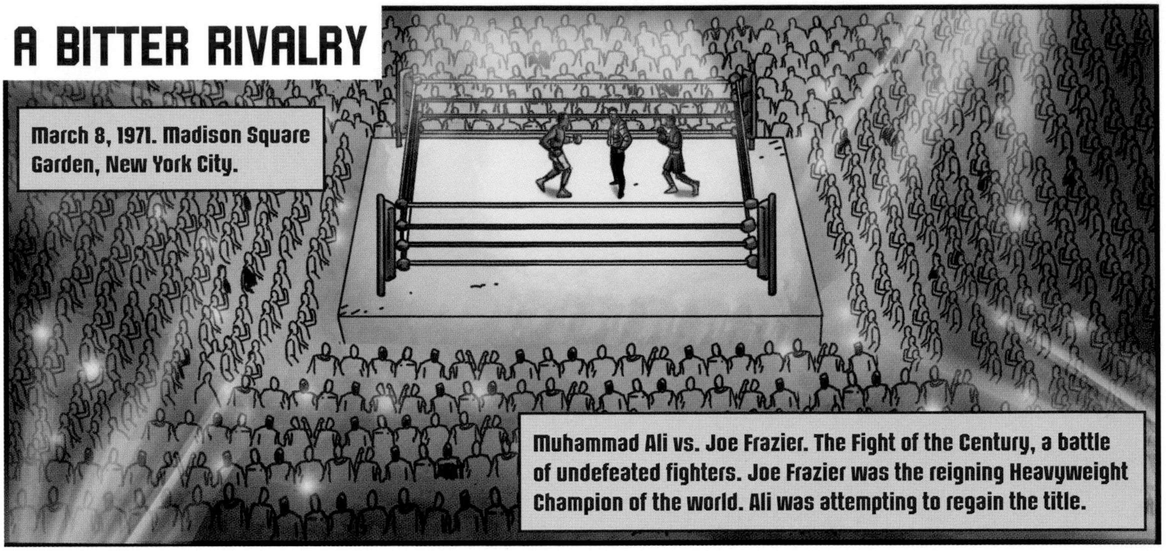
March 8, 1971. Madison Square Garden, New York City.
Muhammad Ali vs. Joe Frazier. The Fight of the Century, a battle of undefeated fighters. Joe Frazier was the reigning Heavyweight Champion of the world. Ali was attempting to regain the title.

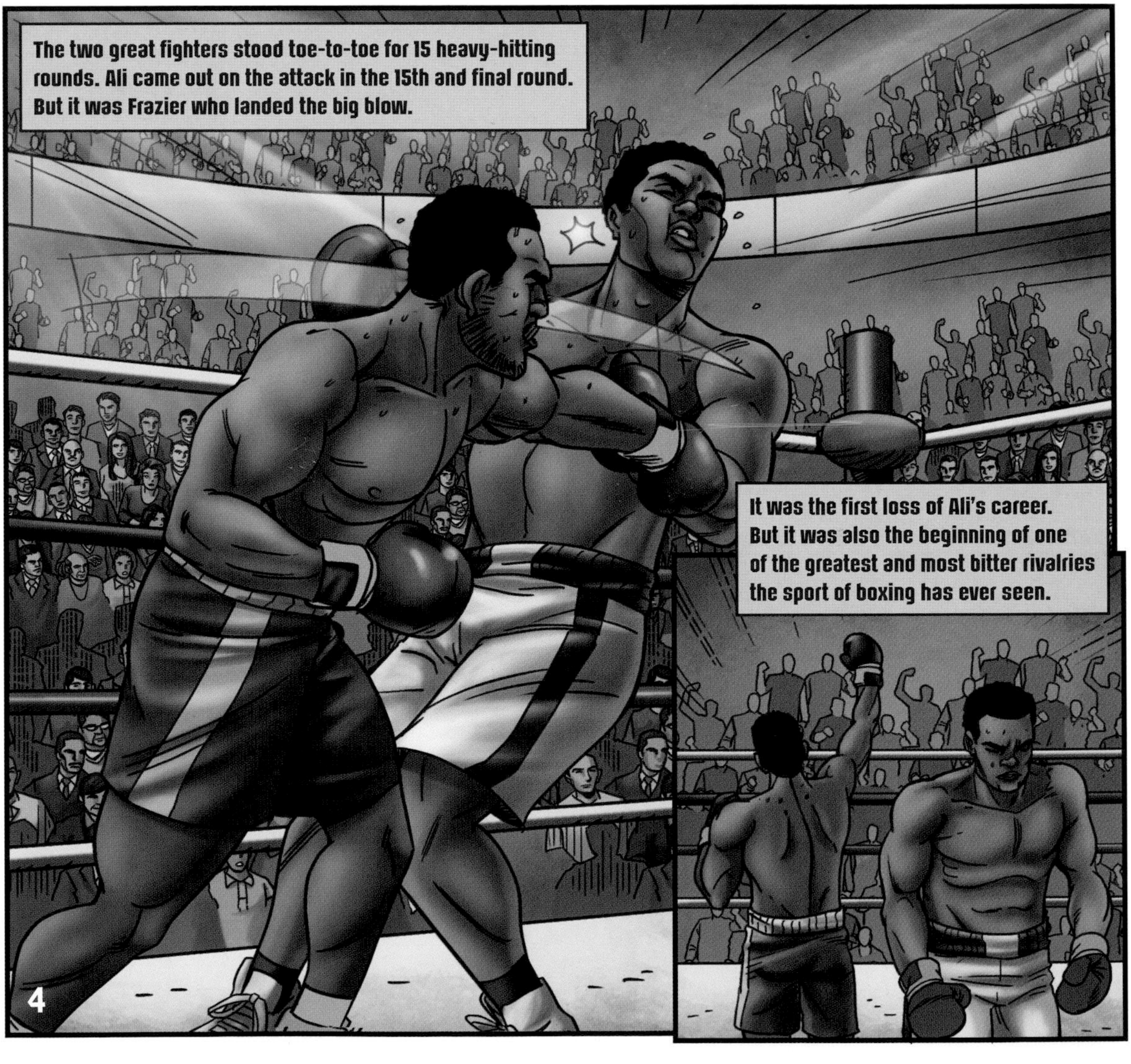
The two great fighters stood toe-to-toe for 15 heavy-hitting rounds. Ali came out on the attack in the 15th and final round. But it was Frazier who landed the big blow.
It was the first loss of Ali's career. But it was also the beginning of one of the greatest and most bitter rivalries the sport of boxing has ever seen.

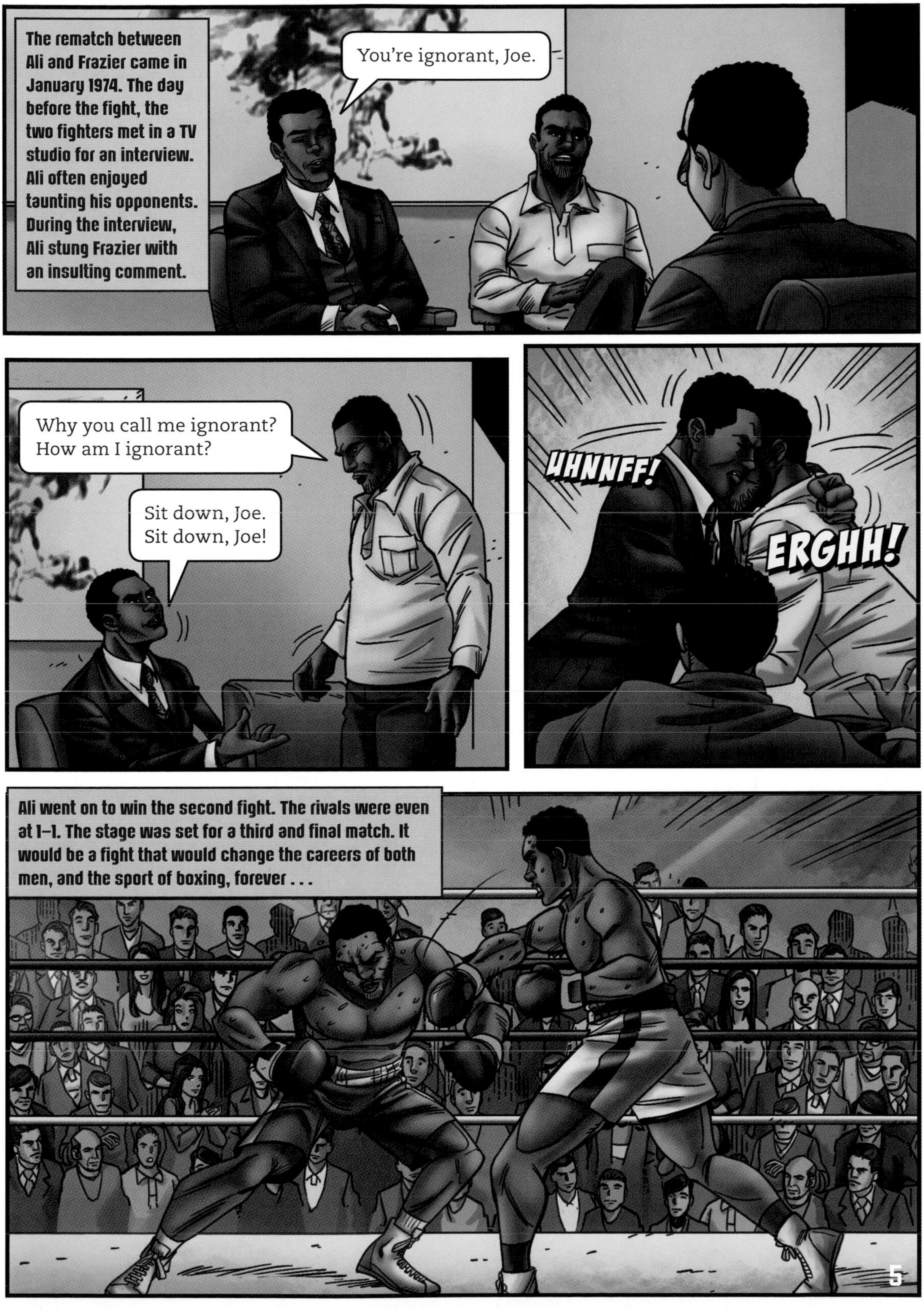
The rematch between Ali and Frazier came in January 1974. The day before the fight, the two fighters met in a TV studio for an interview. Ali often enjoyed taunting his opponents. During the interview, Ali stung Frazier with an insulting comment.
You're ignorant, Joe.
Why you call me ignorant? How am I ignorant?
Sit down, Joe. Sit down, Joe!
UHNNFF!
ERGHH!
Ali went on to win the second fight. The rivals were even at 1–1. The stage was set for a third and final match. It would be a fight that would change the careers of both men, and the sport of boxing, forever . . .

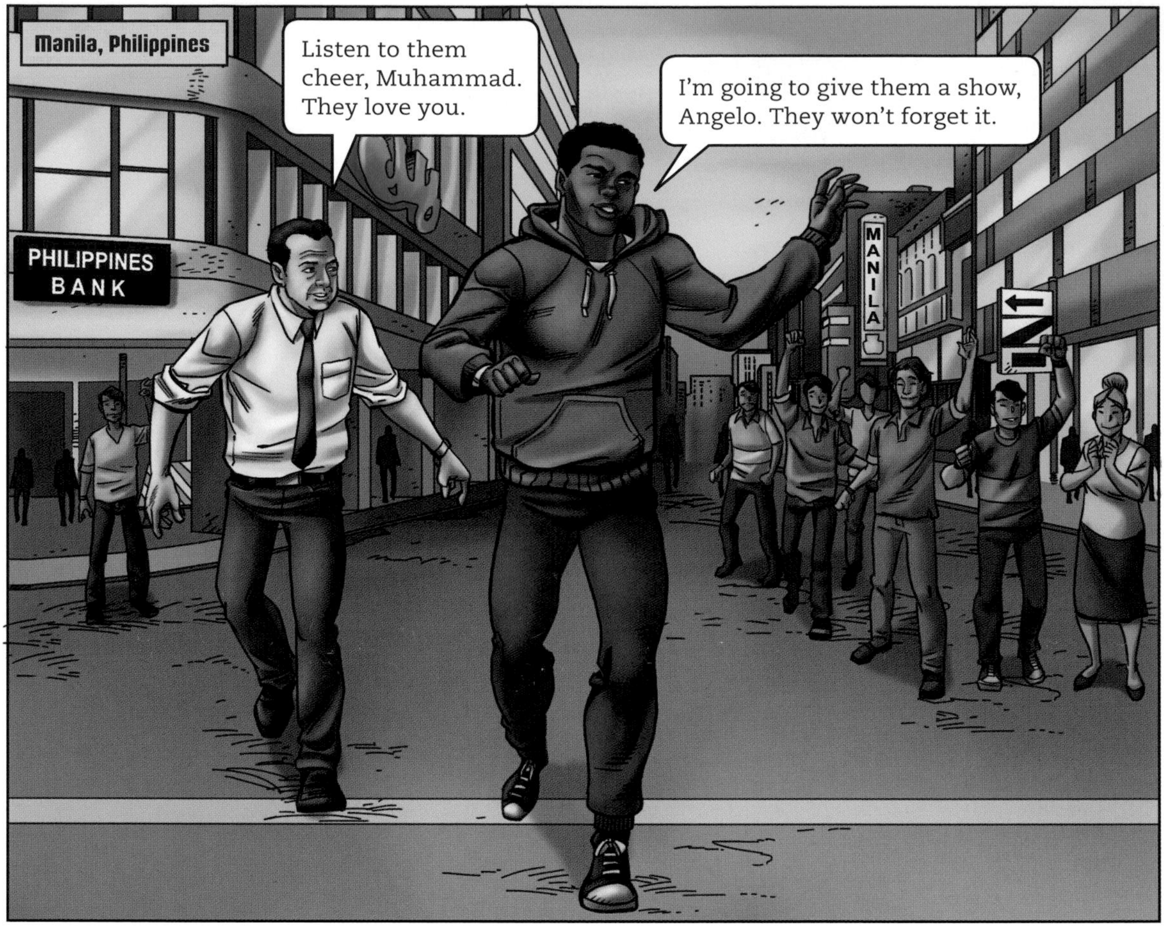
Manila, Philippines
Listen to them cheer, Muhammad. They love you.
I'm going to give them a show, Angelo. They won't forget it.
PHILIPPINES BANK
MANILA

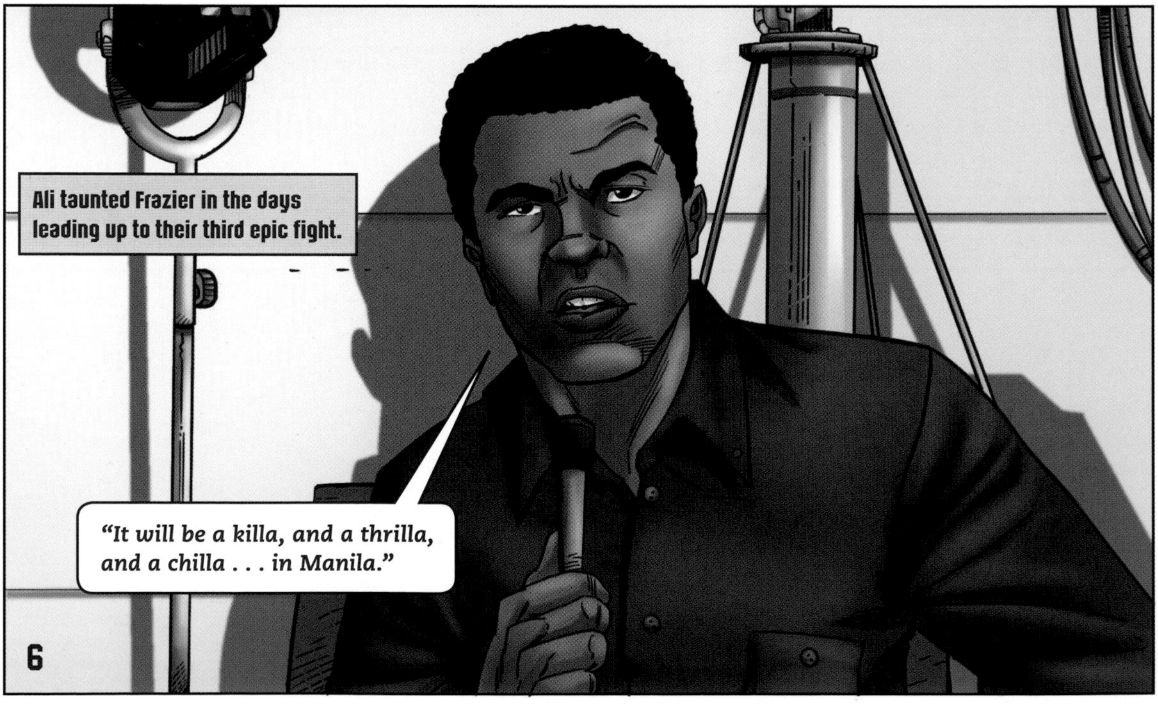
Ali taunted Frazier in the days leading up to their third epic fight.
"It will be a killa, and a thrilla, and a chilla . . . in Manila."

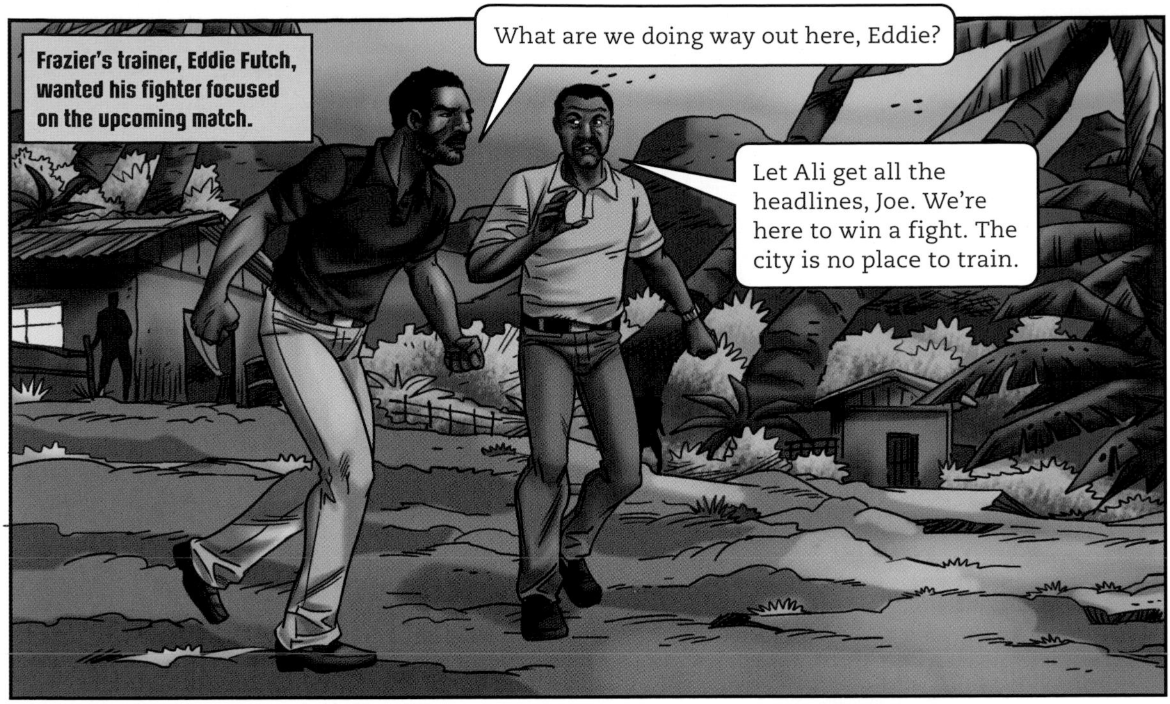

Frazier's trainer, Eddie Futch, wanted his fighter focused on the upcoming match.
What are we doing way out here, Eddie?
Let Ali get all the headlines, Joe. We're here to win a fight. The city is no place to train.

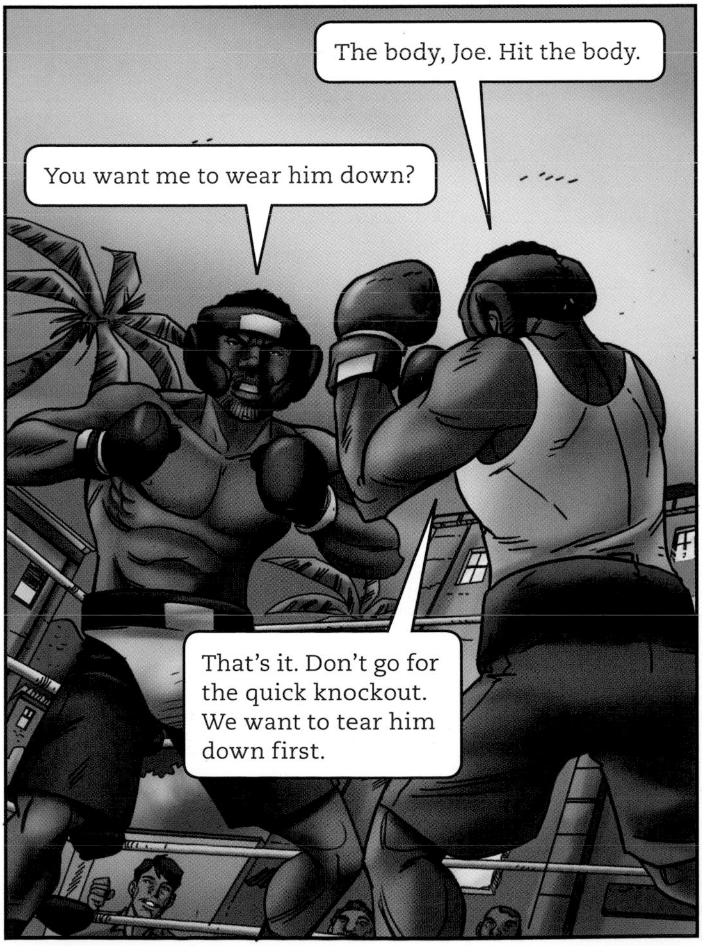

You want me to wear him down?
The body, Joe. Hit the body.
That's it. Don't go for the quick knockout. We want to tear him down first.

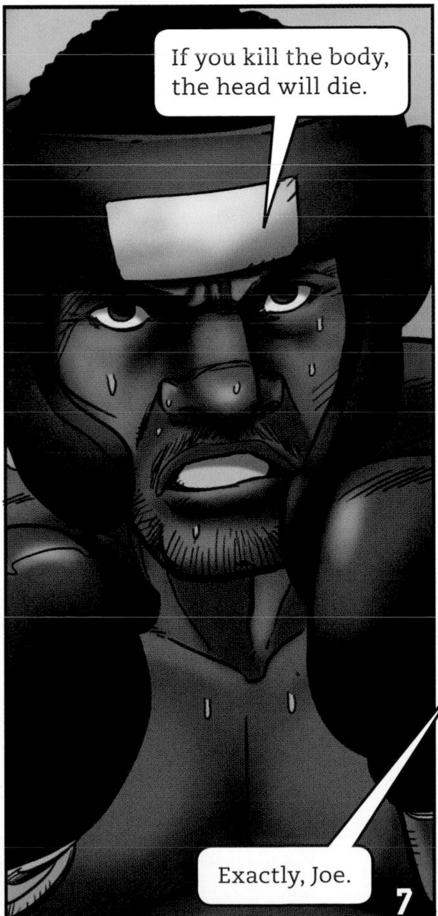

If you kill the body, the head will die.
Exactly, Joe.

THE SHOWDOWN BEGINS

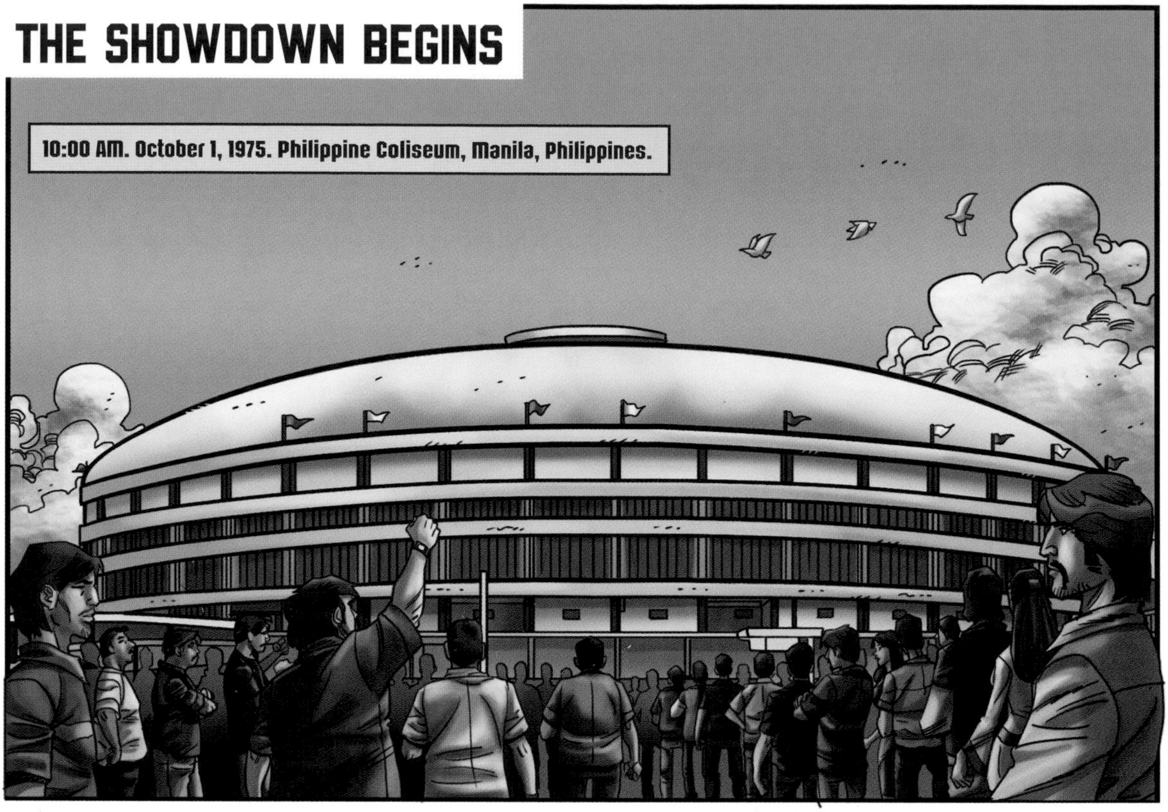
10:00 AM. October 1, 1975. Philippine Coliseum, Manila, Philippines.

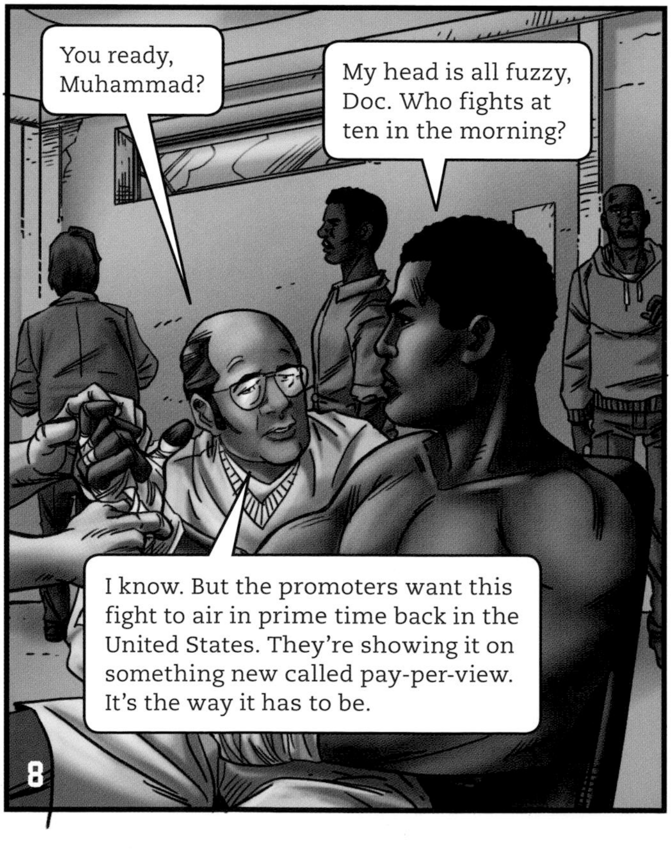
You ready, Muhammad?
My head is all fuzzy, Doc. Who fights at ten in the morning?
I know. But the promoters want this fight to air in prime time back in the United States. They're showing it on something new called pay-per-view. It's the way it has to be.

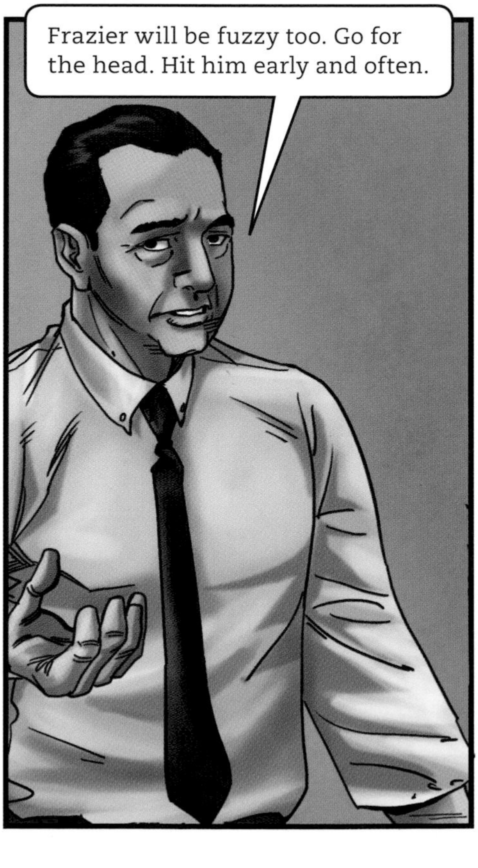
Frazier will be fuzzy too. Go for the head. Hit him early and often.

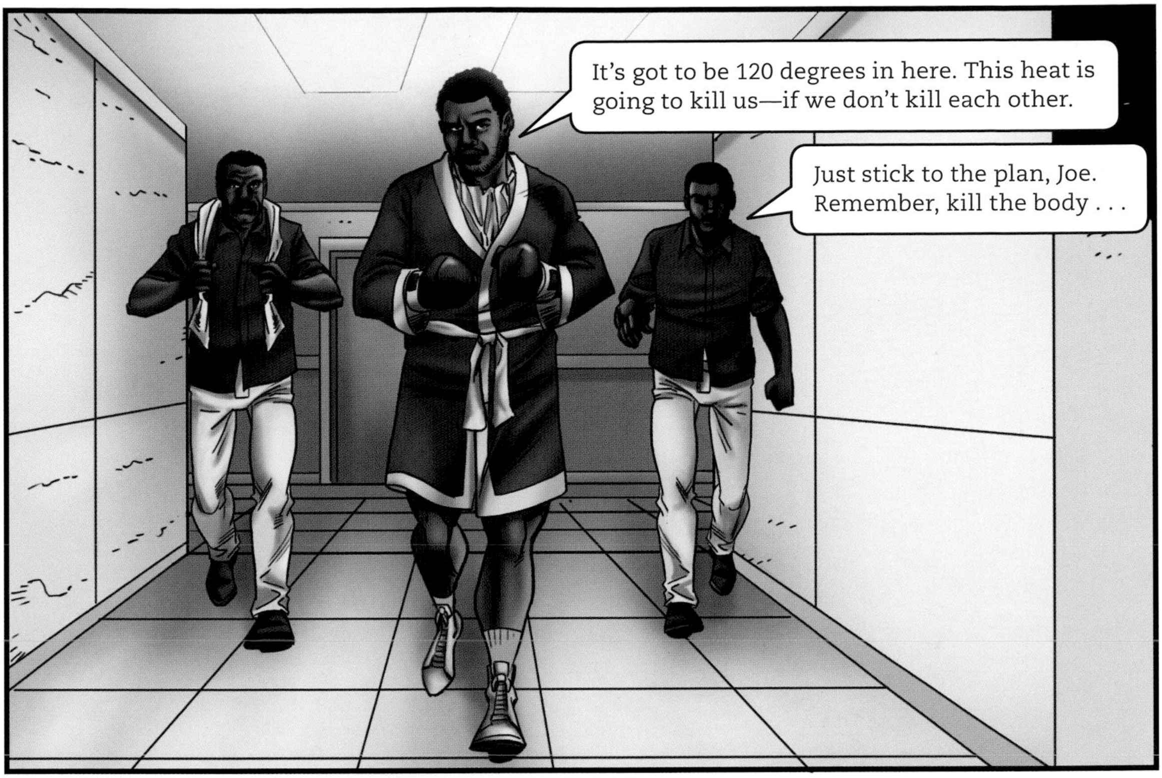
It's got to be 120 degrees in here. This heat is going to kill us—if we don't kill each other.
Just stick to the plan, Joe. Remember, kill the body . . .

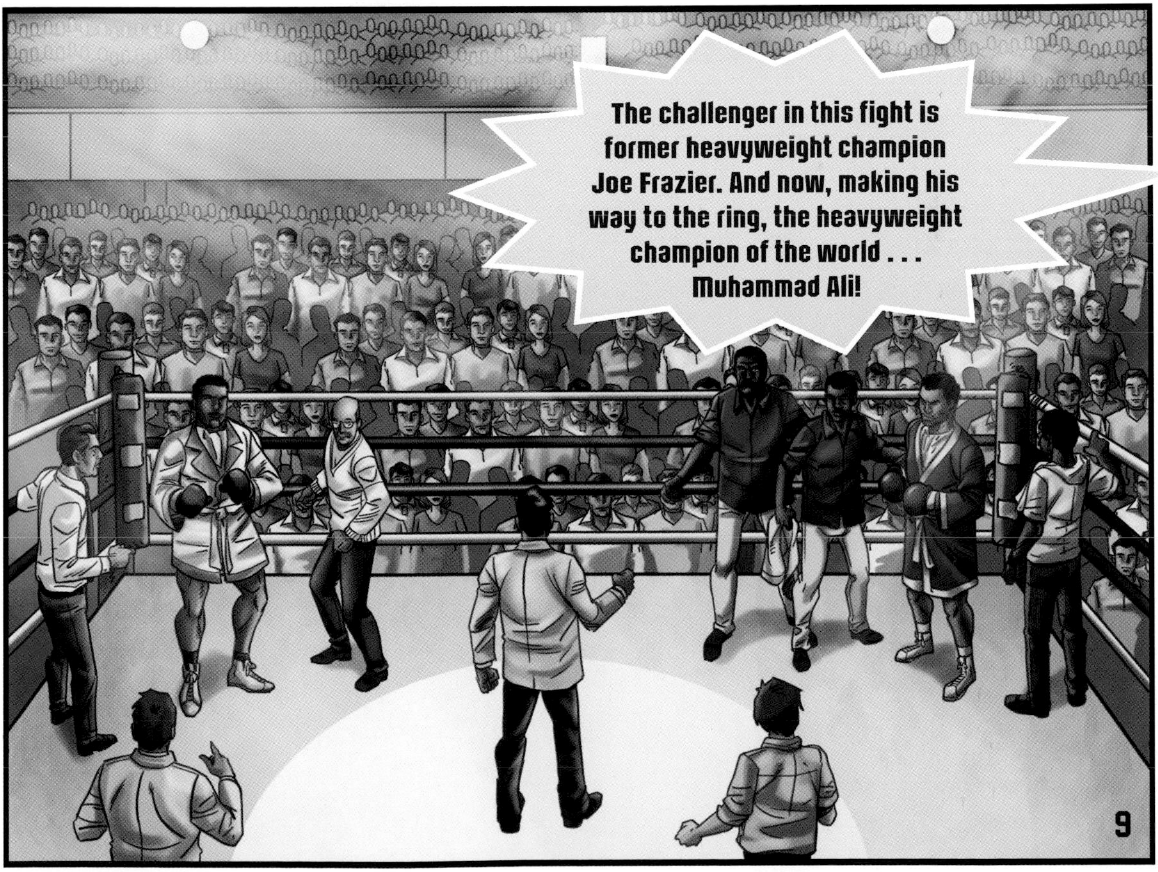
The challenger in this fight is former heavyweight champion Joe Frazier. And now, making his way to the ring, the heavyweight champion of the world . . . Muhammad Ali!

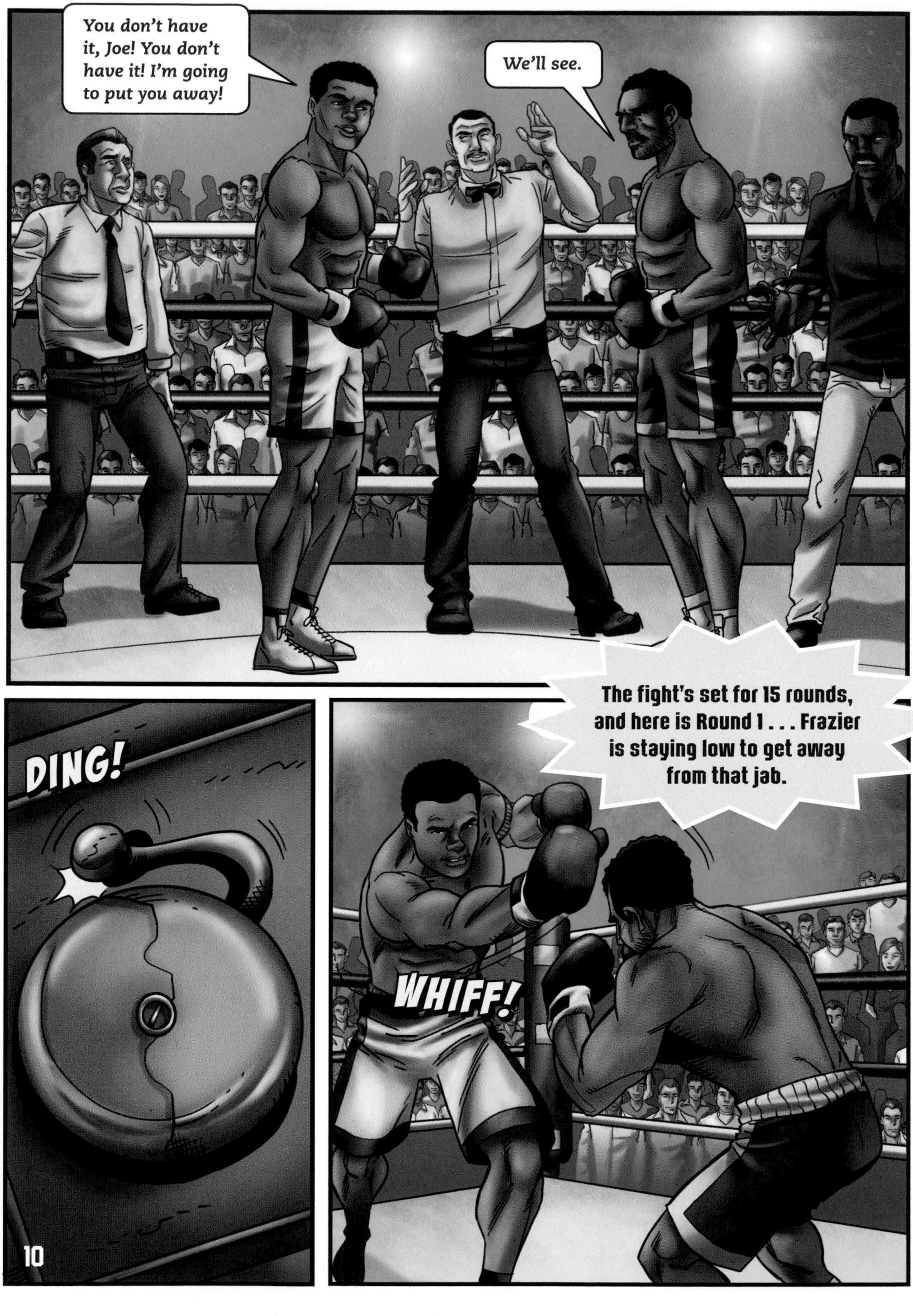
You don't have it, Joe! You don't have it! I'm going to put you away!
We'll see.
DING!
The fight's set for 15 rounds, and here is Round 1 . . . Frazier is staying low to get away from that jab.
WHIFF!

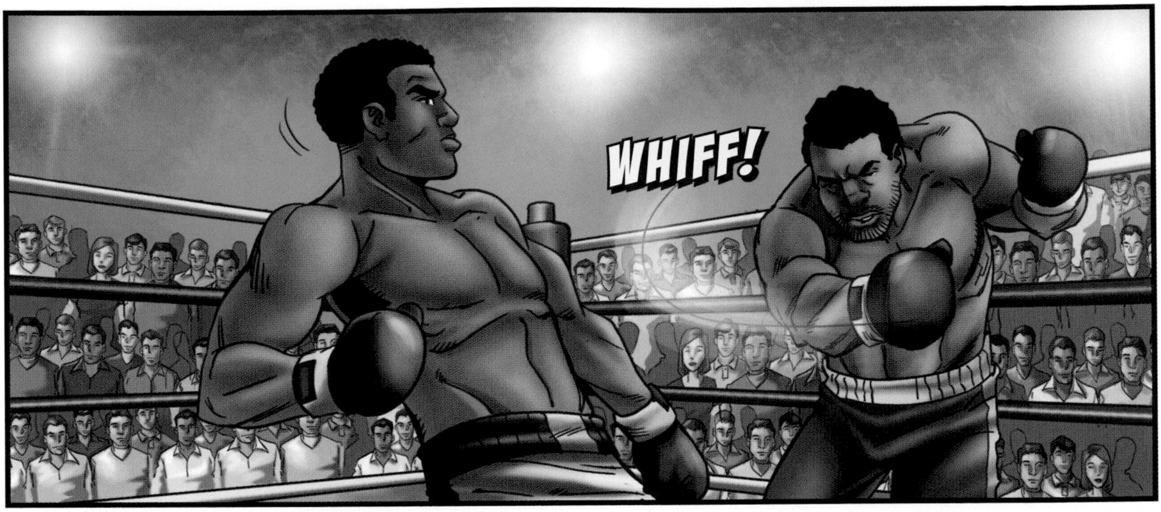
WHIFF!

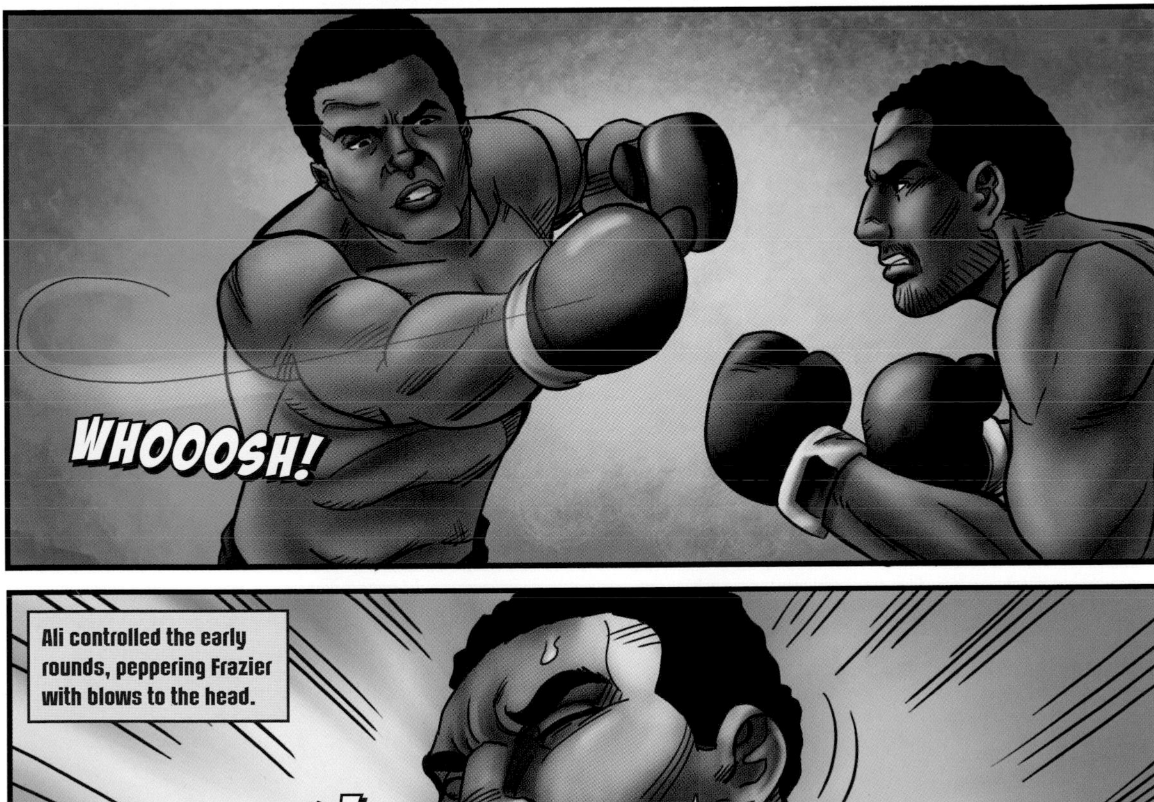
WHOOOSH!

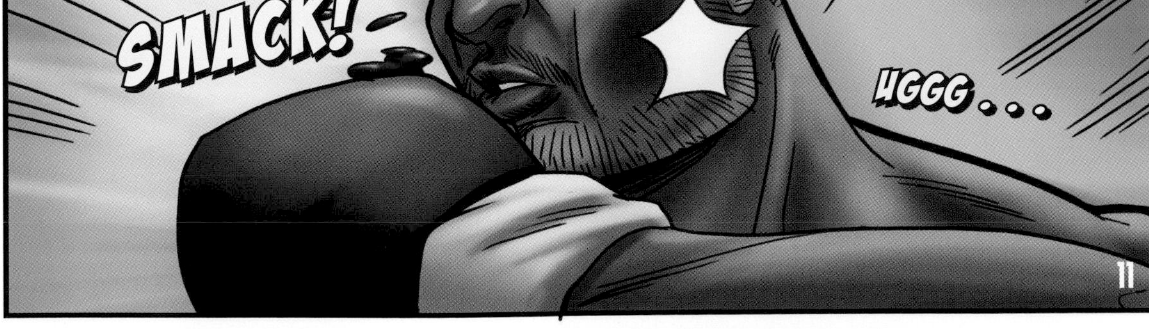
Ali controlled the early rounds, peppering Frazier with blows to the head.
SMACK!
UGGG . . .

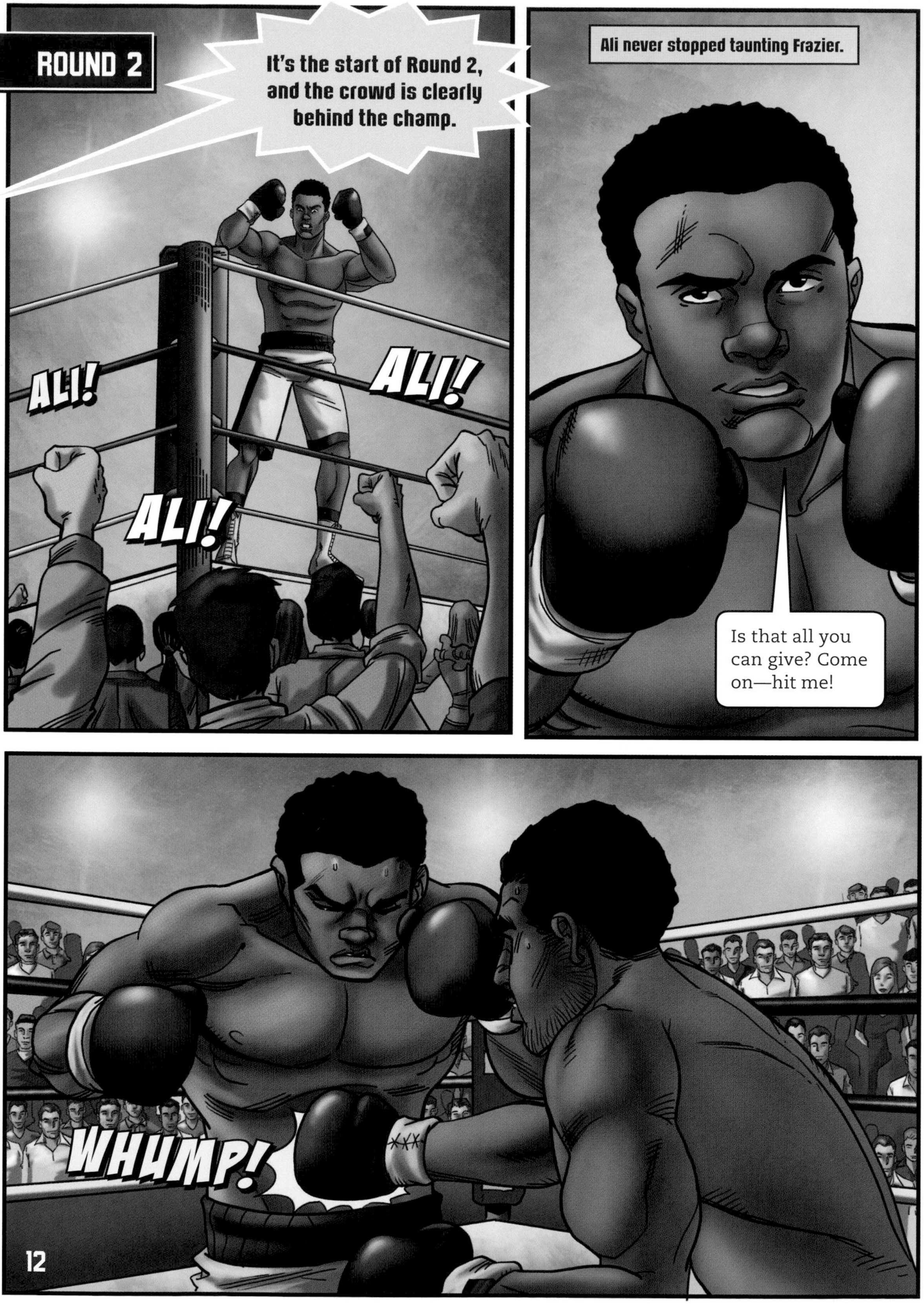
ROUND 2
It's the start of Round 2, and the crowd is clearly behind the champ.
ALI!
ALI!
ALI!
Ali never stopped taunting Frazier.
Is that all you can give? Come on—hit me!
WHUMP!

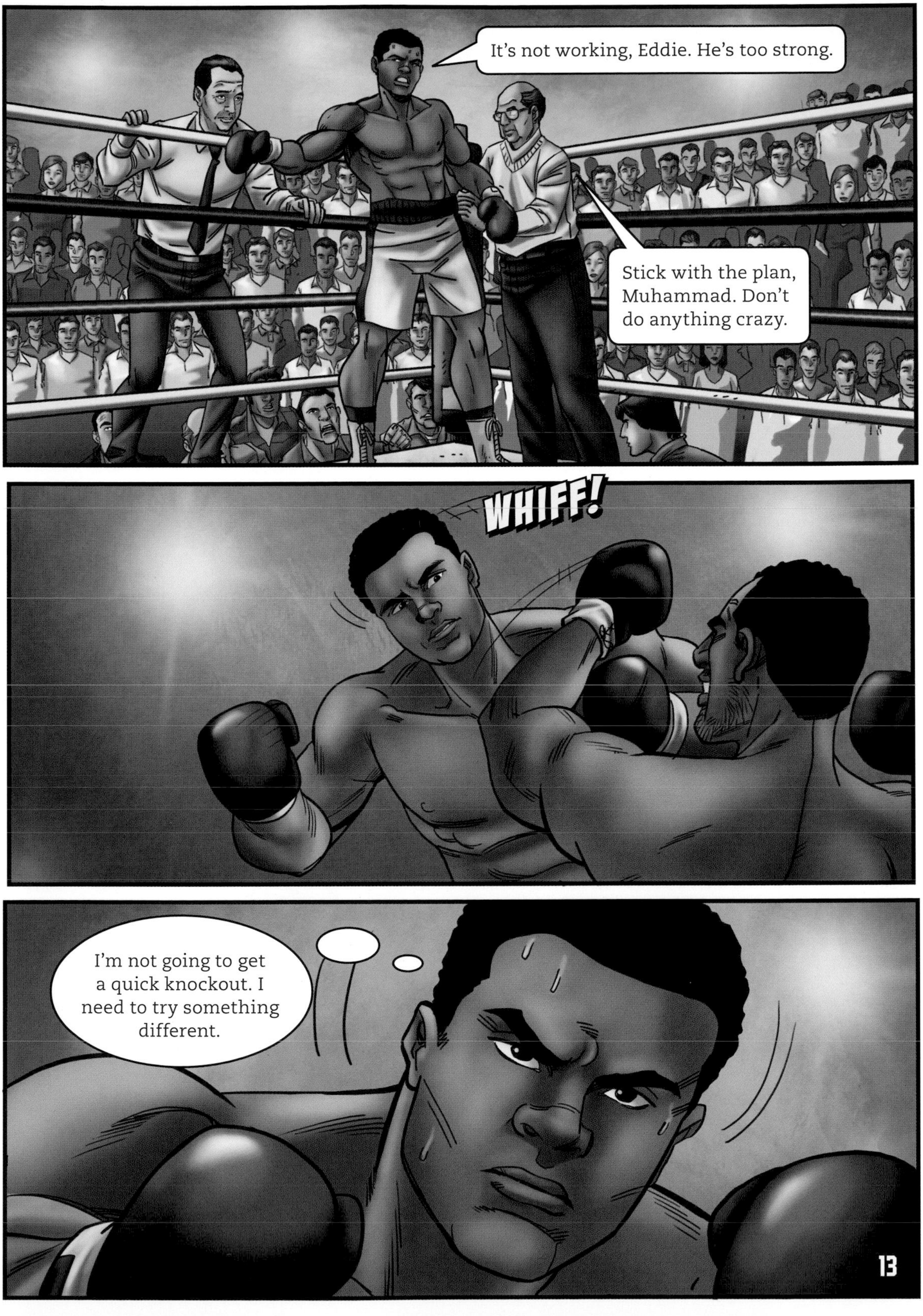
It's not working, Eddie. He's too strong.
Stick with the plan, Muhammad. Don't do anything crazy.
WHIFF!
I'm not going to get a quick knockout. I need to try something different.

CHANGING TACTICS

ROUND 3

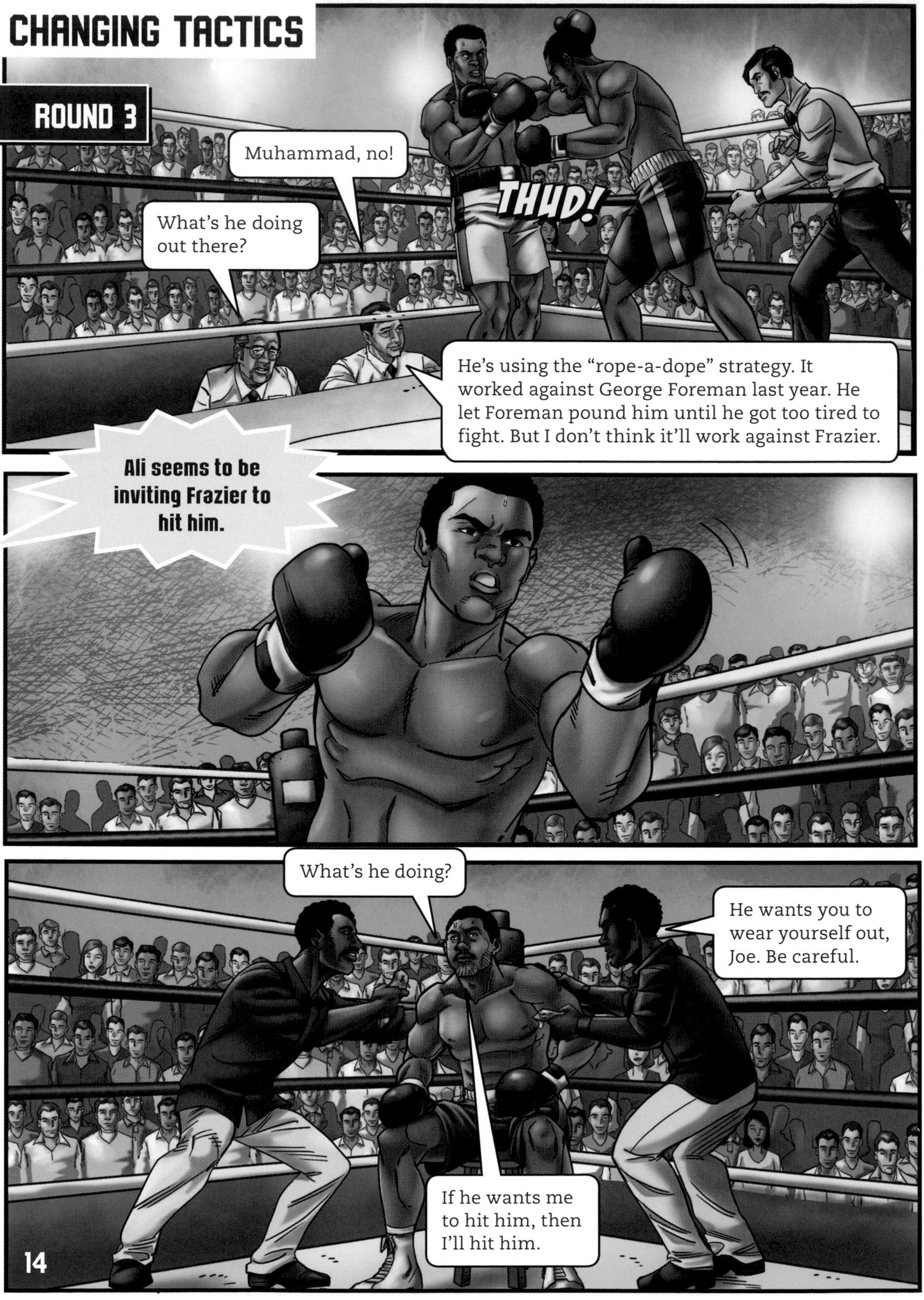

Muhammad, no!
What's he doing out there?
THUD!
He's using the "rope-a-dope" strategy. It worked against George Foreman last year. He let Foreman pound him until he got too tired to fight. But I don't think it'll work against Frazier.
Ali seems to be inviting Frazier to hit him.
What's he doing?
He wants you to wear yourself out, Joe. Be careful.
If he wants me to hit him, then I'll hit him.

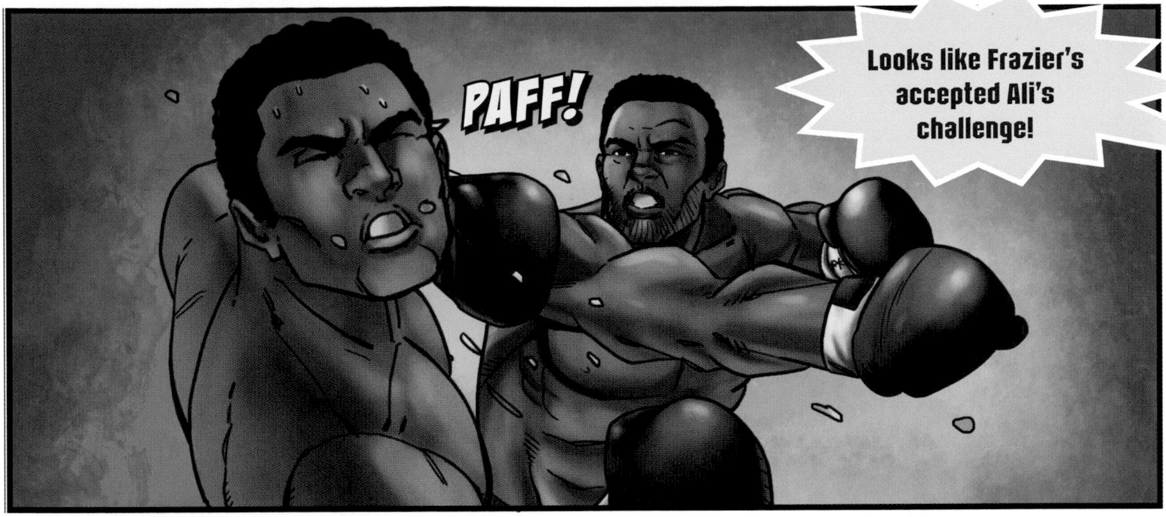
PAFF!
Looks like Frazier's accepted Ali's challenge!

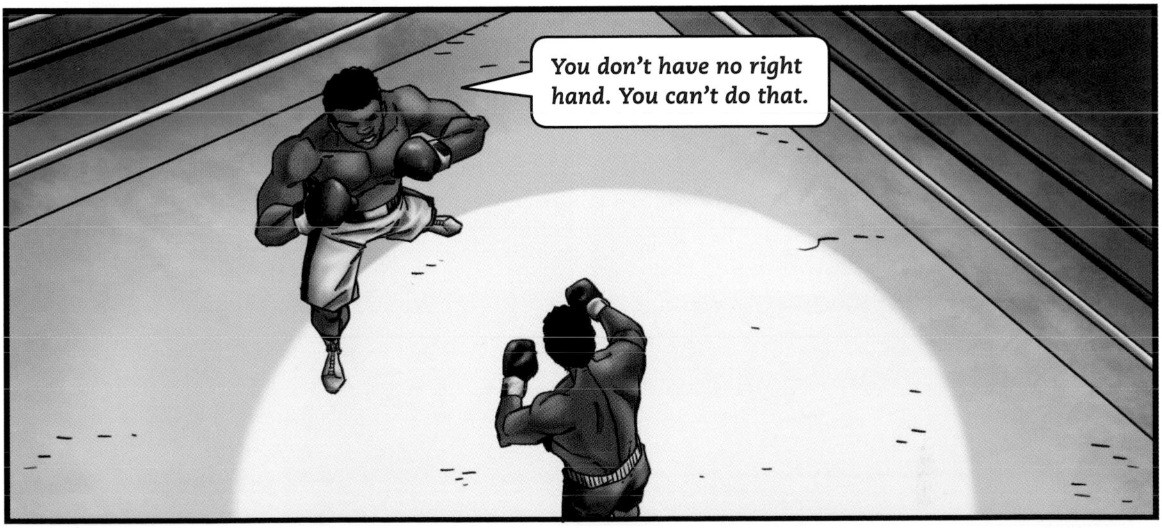
You don't have no right hand. You can't do that.

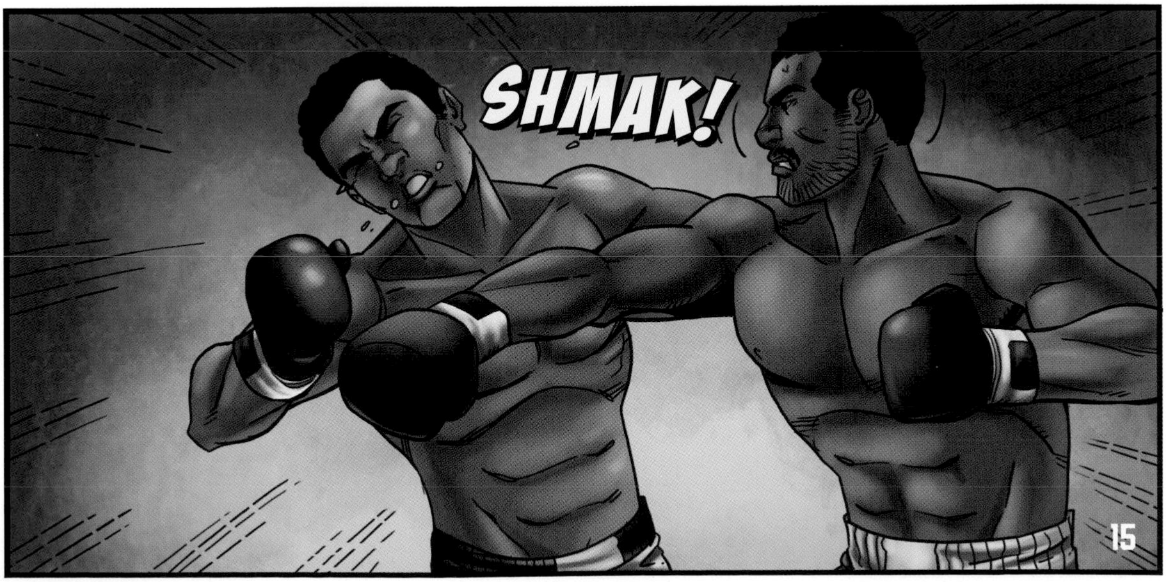
SHMAK!

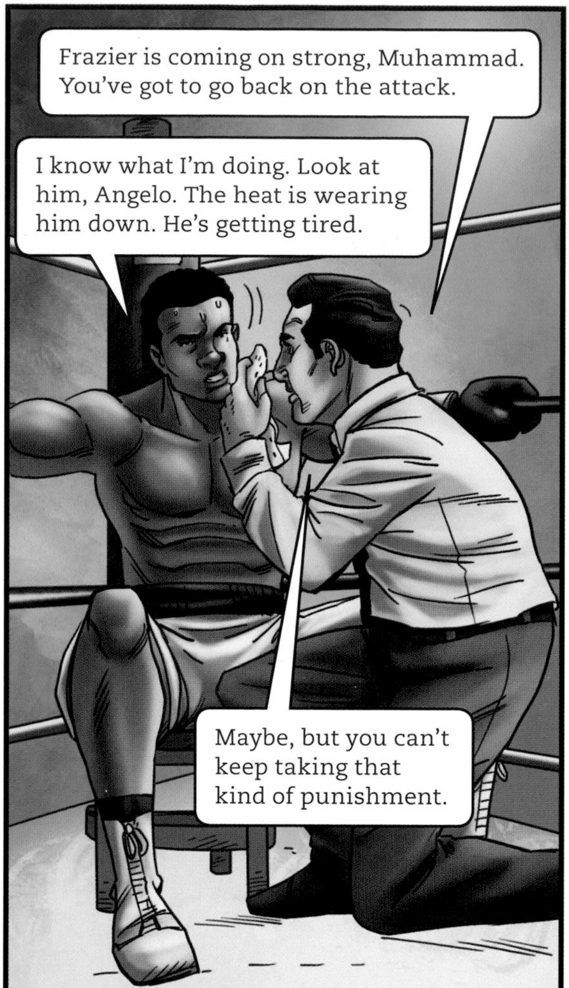
Frazier is coming on strong, Muhammad. You've got to go back on the attack.
I know what I'm doing. Look at him, Angelo. The heat is wearing him down. He's getting tired.
Maybe, but you can't keep taking that kind of punishment.

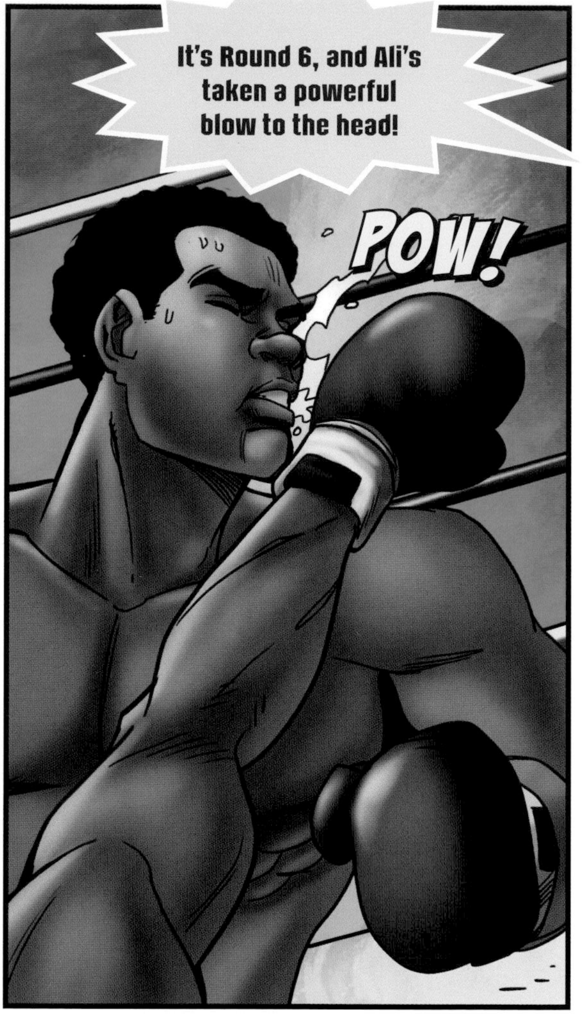
It's Round 6, and Ali's taken a powerful blow to the head!
POW!

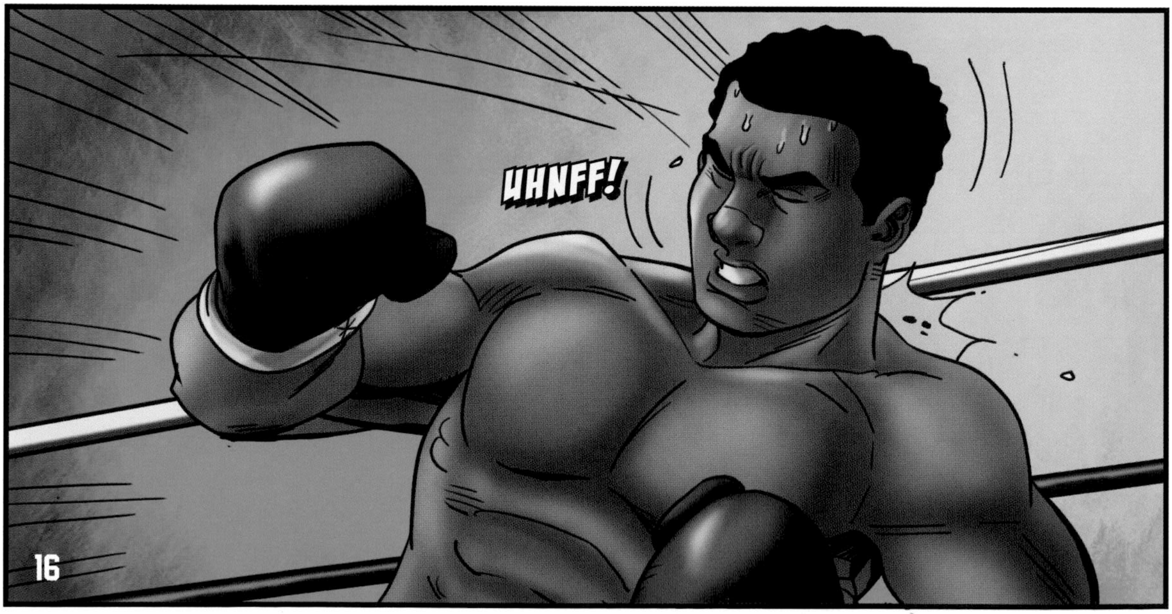
UHNFF!

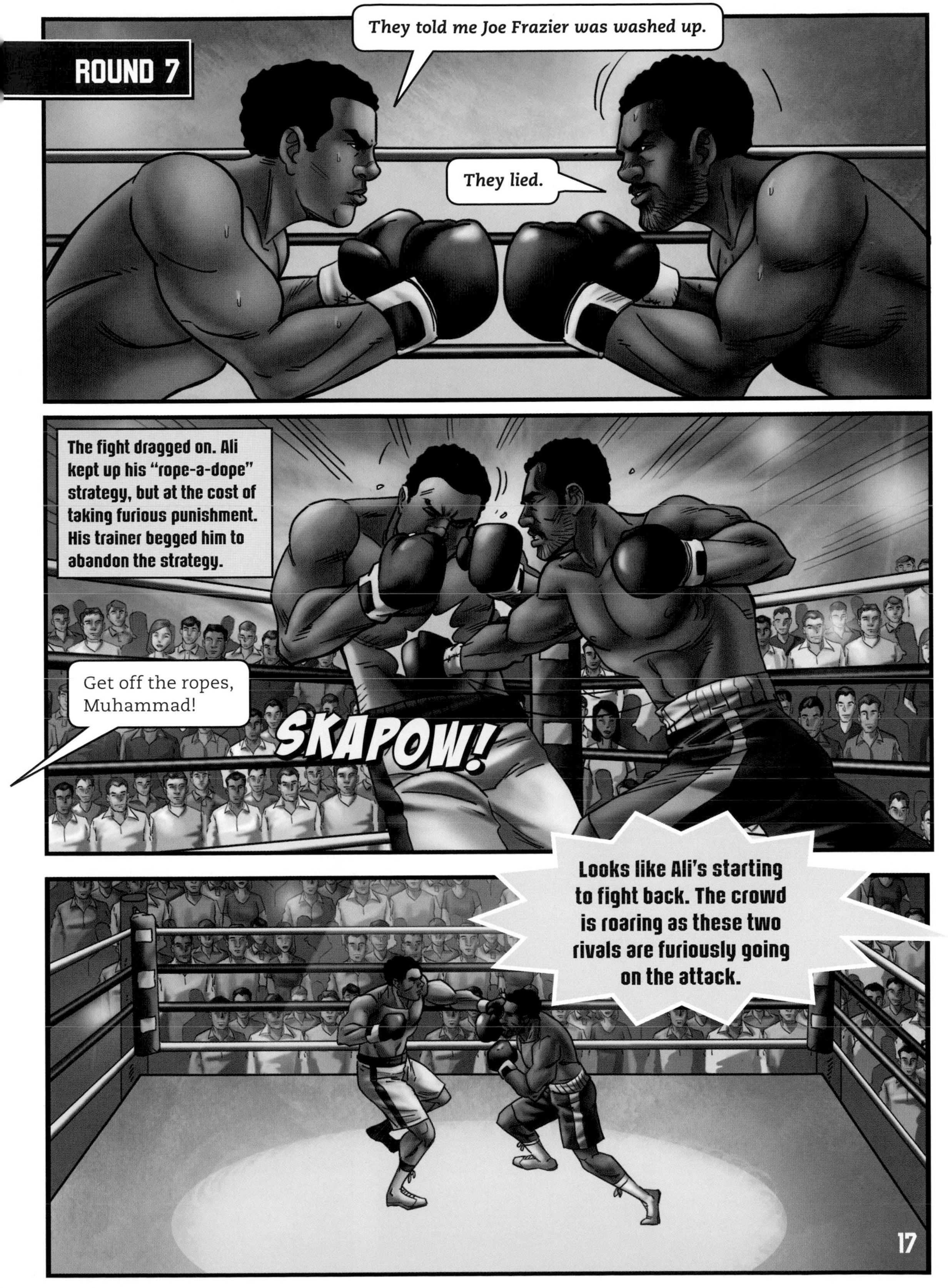
ROUND 7
They told me Joe Frazier was washed up.
They lied.
The fight dragged on. Ali kept up his "rope-a-dope" strategy, but at the cost of taking furious punishment. His trainer begged him to abandon the strategy.
Get off the ropes, Muhammad!
SKAPOW!
Looks like Ali's starting to fight back. The crowd is roaring as these two rivals are furiously going on the attack.

ALI TURNS THE TIDE

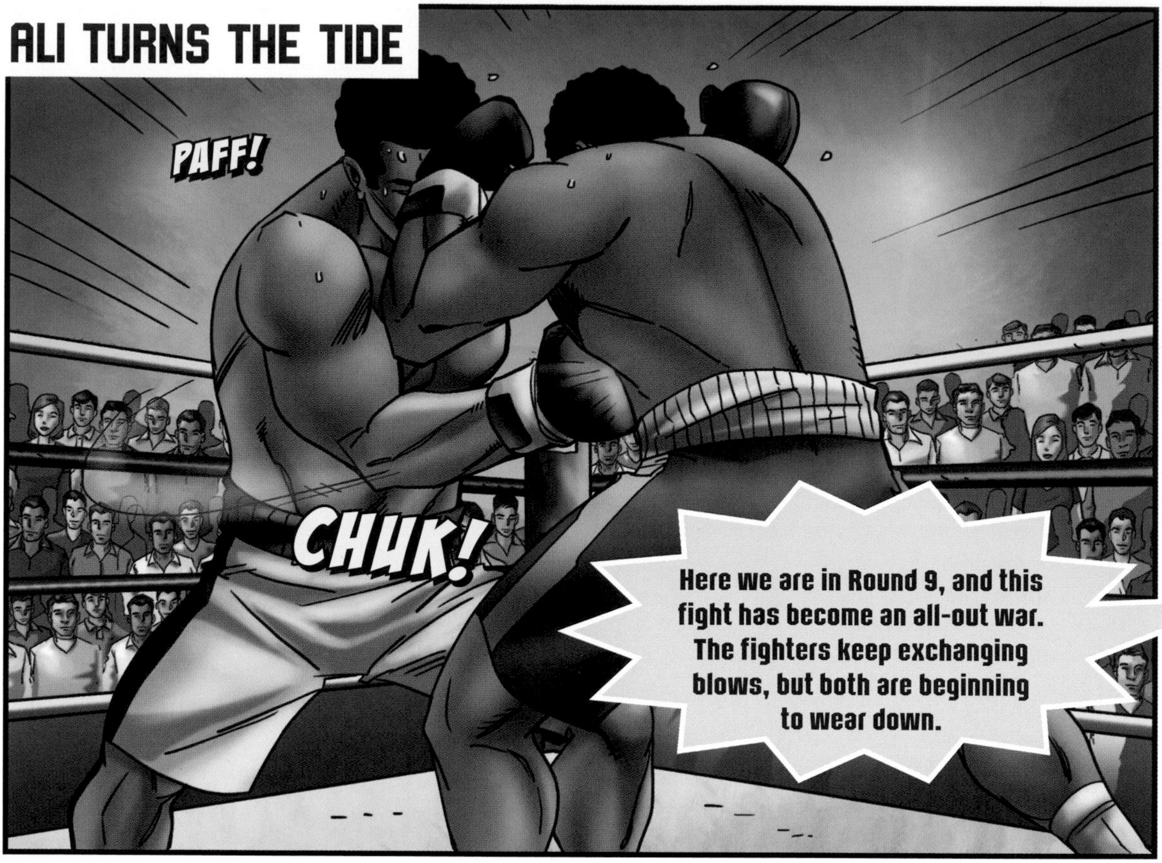
PAFF!
CHUK!
Here we are in Round 9, and this fight has become an all-out war. The fighters keep exchanging blows, but both are beginning to wear down.

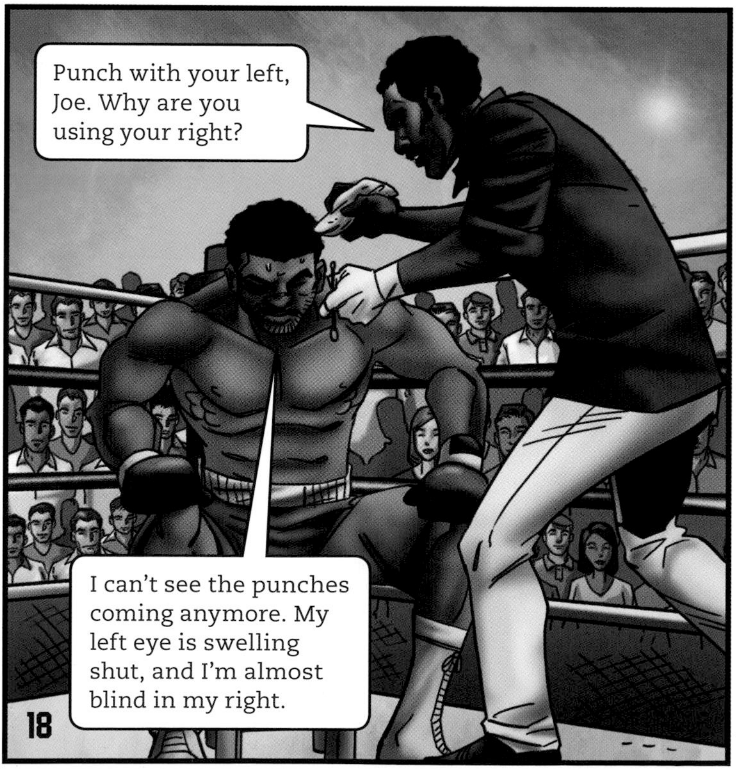
Punch with your left, Joe. Why are you using your right?
I can't see the punches coming anymore. My left eye is swelling shut, and I'm almost blind in my right.

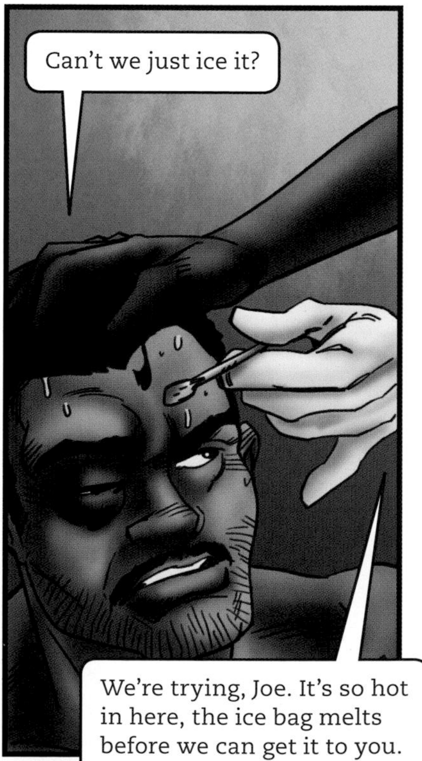
Can't we just ice it?
We're trying, Joe. It's so hot in here, the ice bag melts before we can get it to you.

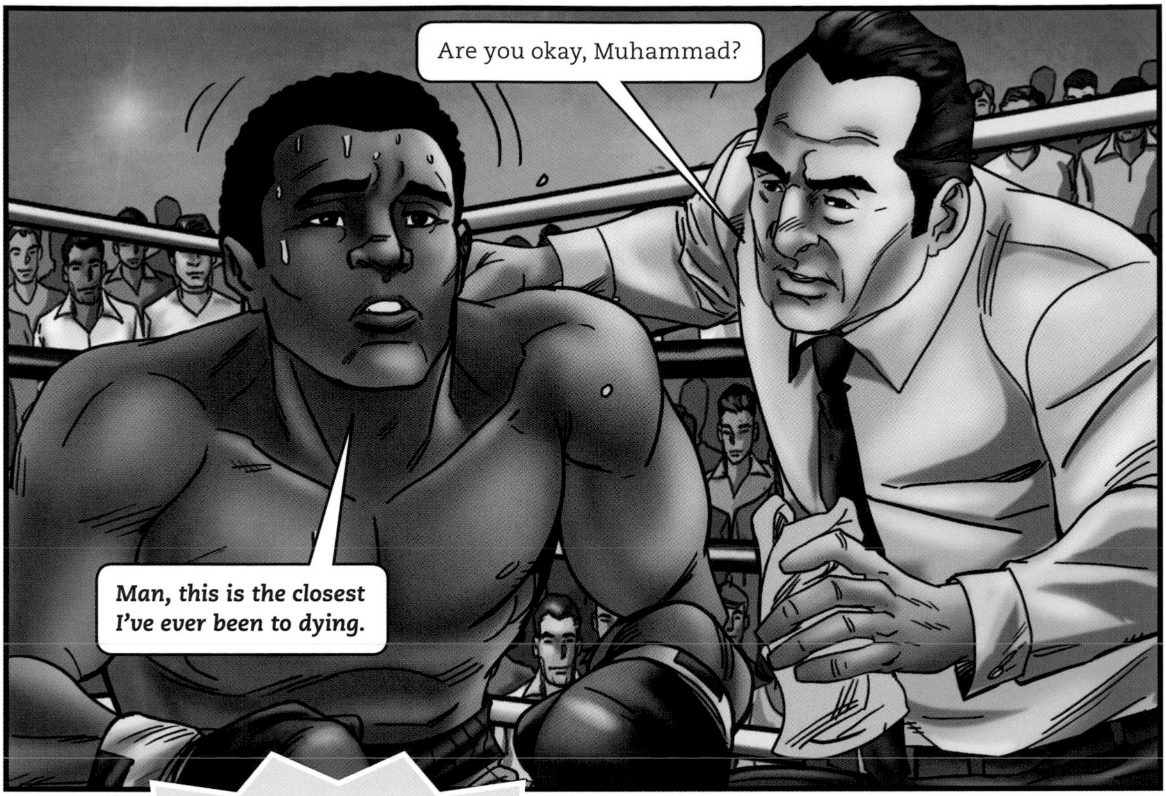
Are you okay, Muhammad?
Man, this is the closest I've ever been to dying.

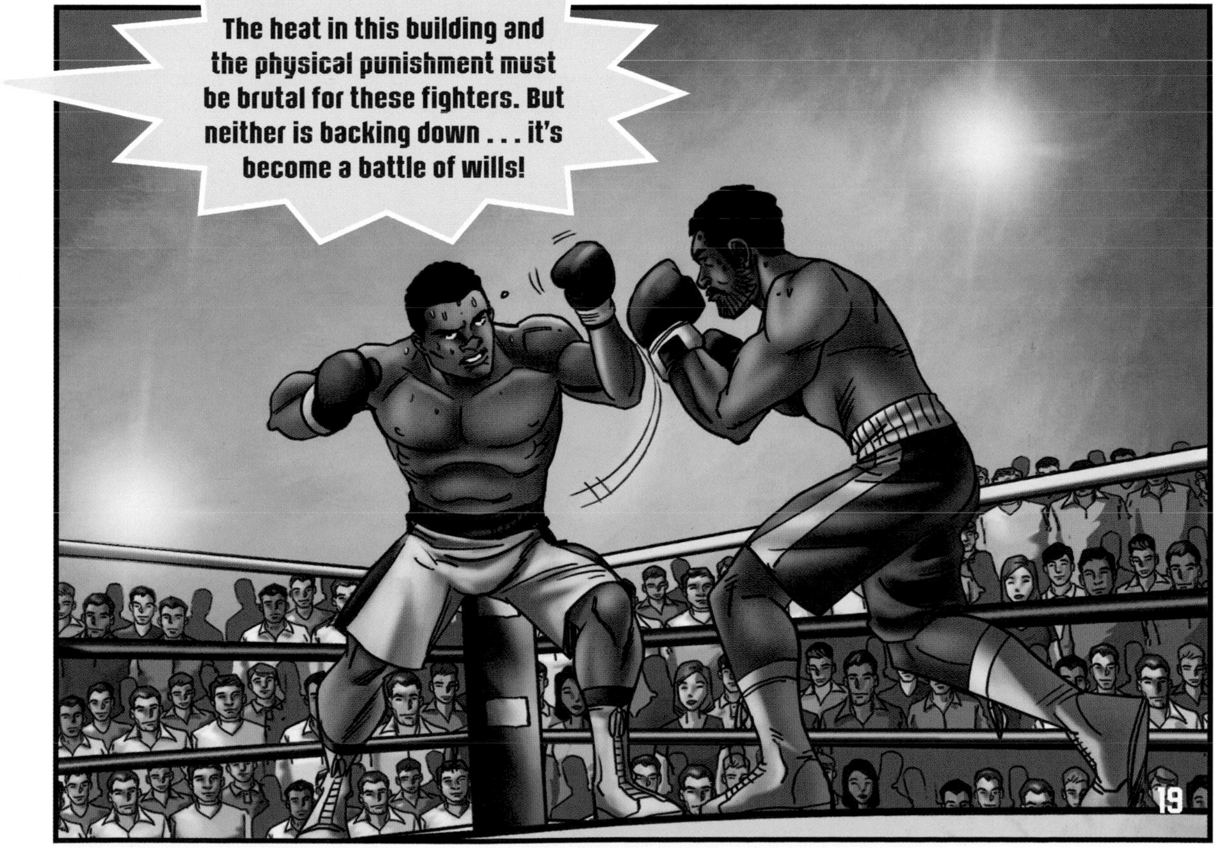
The heat in this building and the physical punishment must be brutal for these fighters. But neither is backing down . . . it's become a battle of wills!

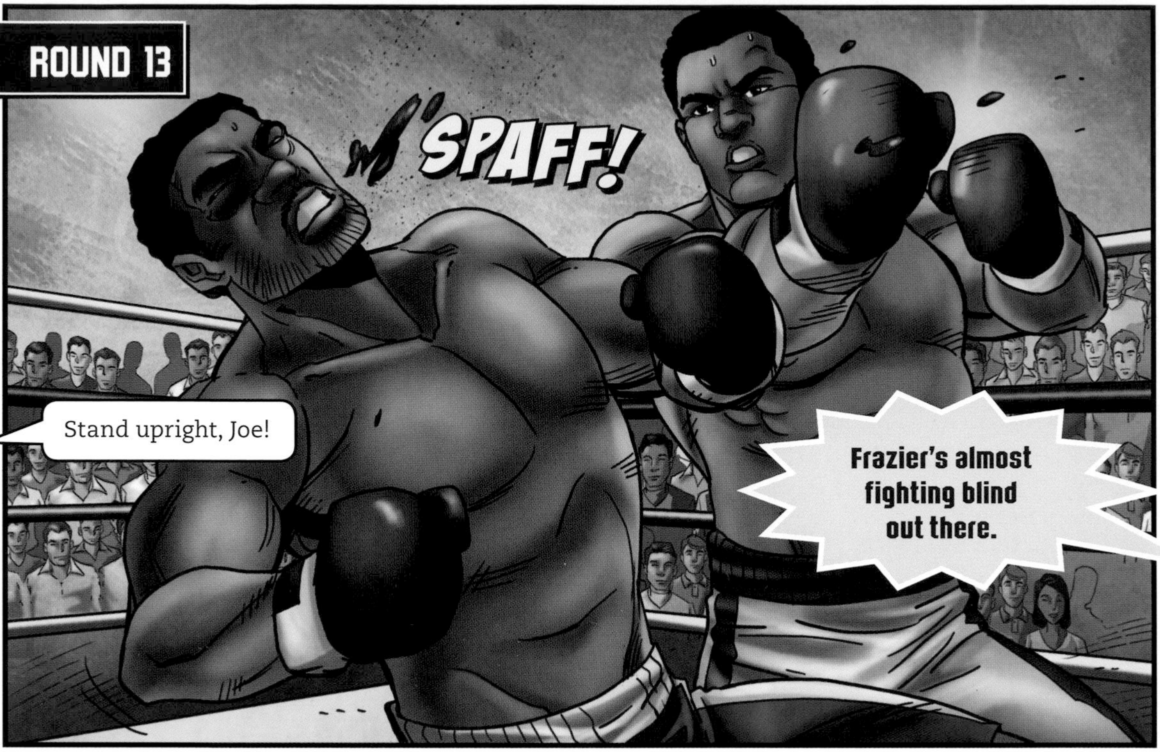
ROUND 13
SPAFF!
Stand upright, Joe!
Frazier's almost fighting blind out there.

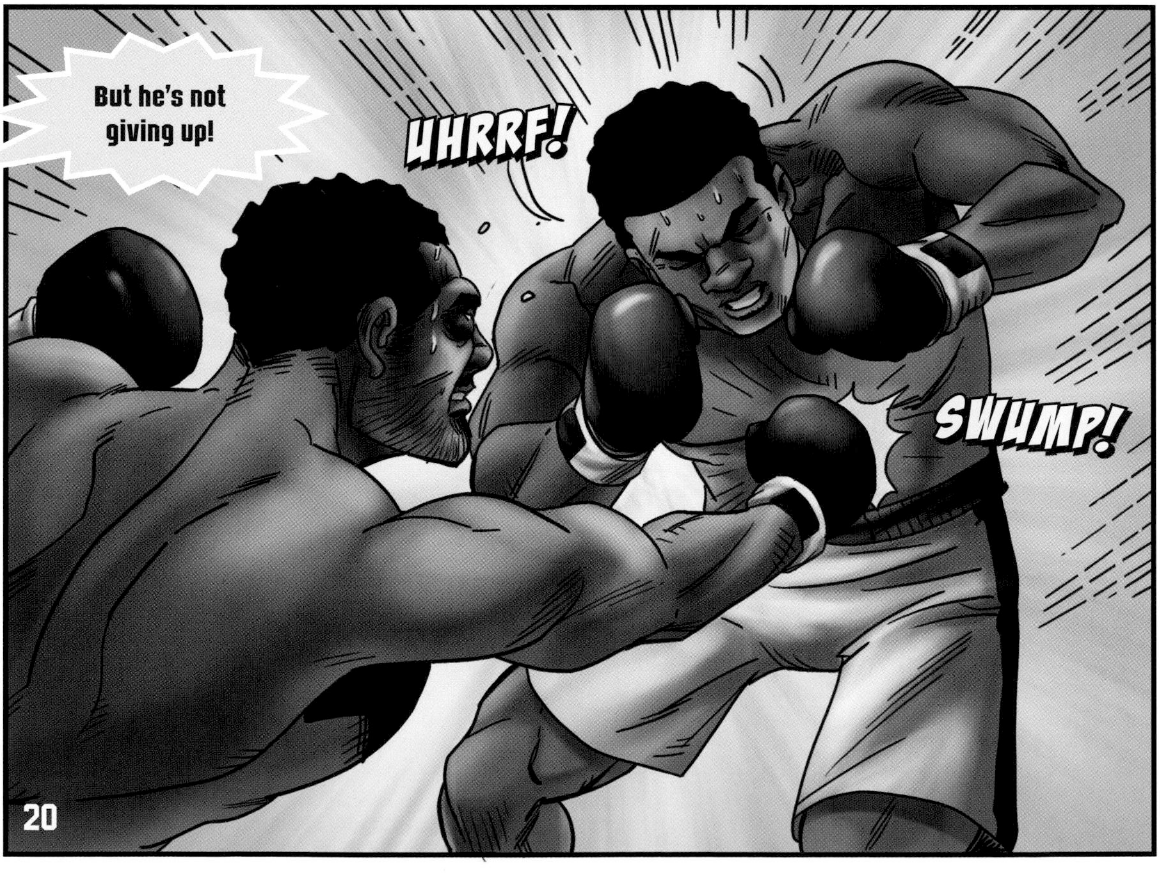
But he's not giving up!
UHRRF!
SWUMP!

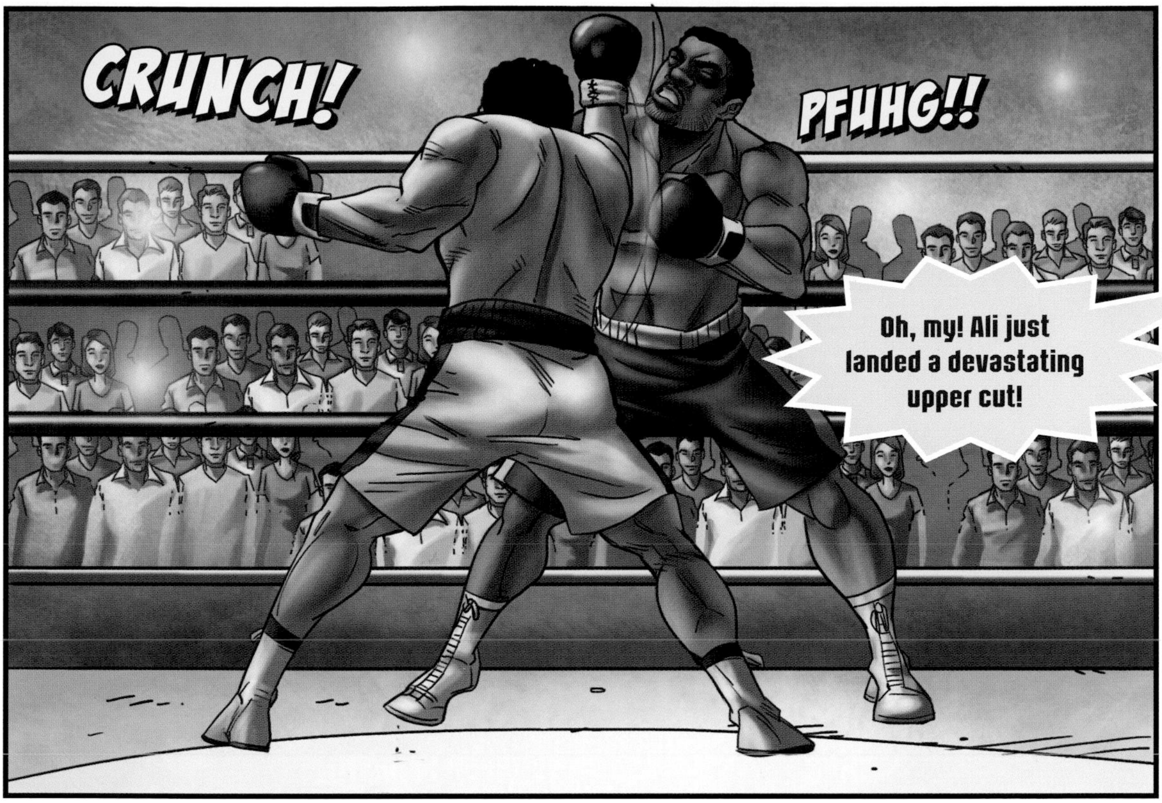
CRUNCH!
PFUHG!!
Oh, my! Ali just landed a devastating upper cut!

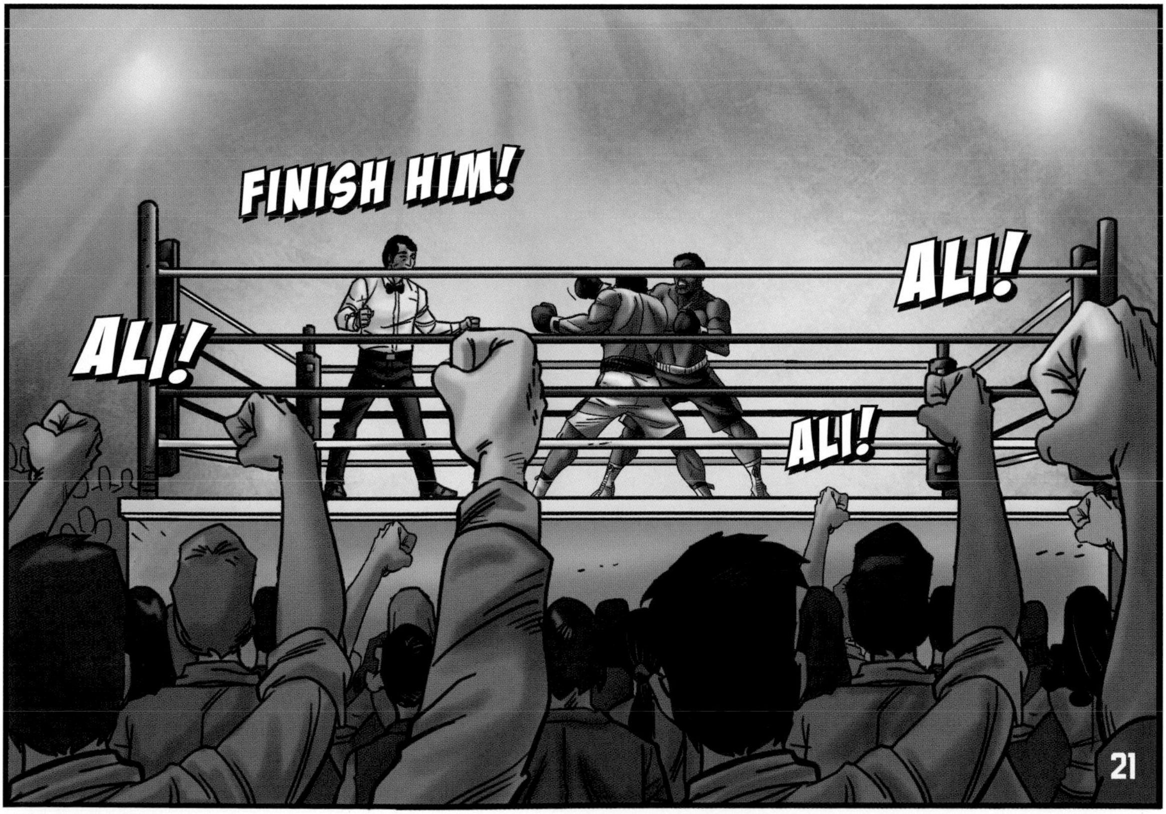
FINISH HIM!
ALI!
ALI!
ALI!

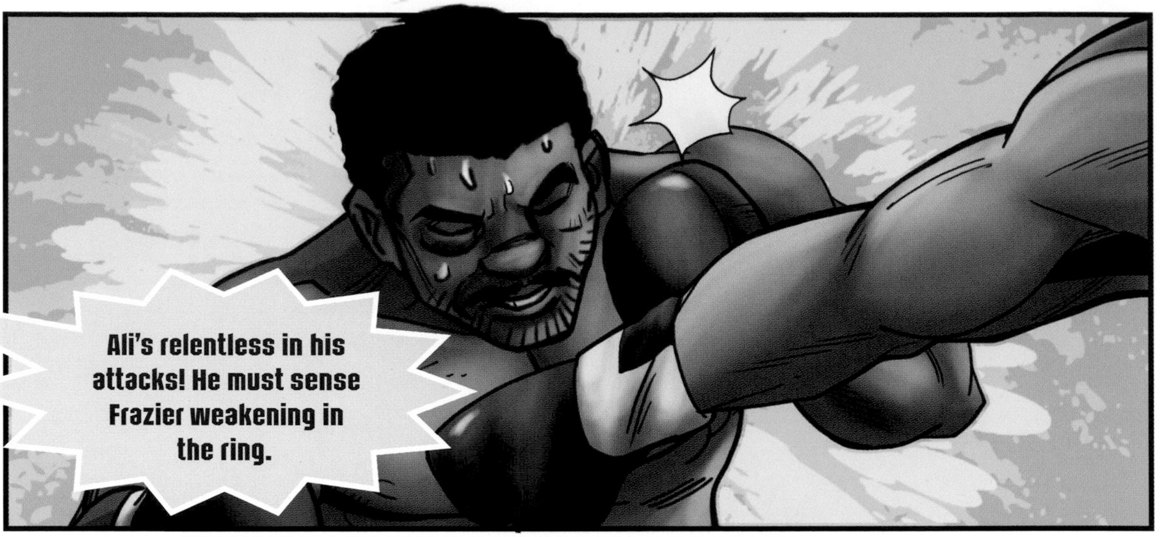
Ali's relentless in his attacks! He must sense Frazier weakening in the ring.

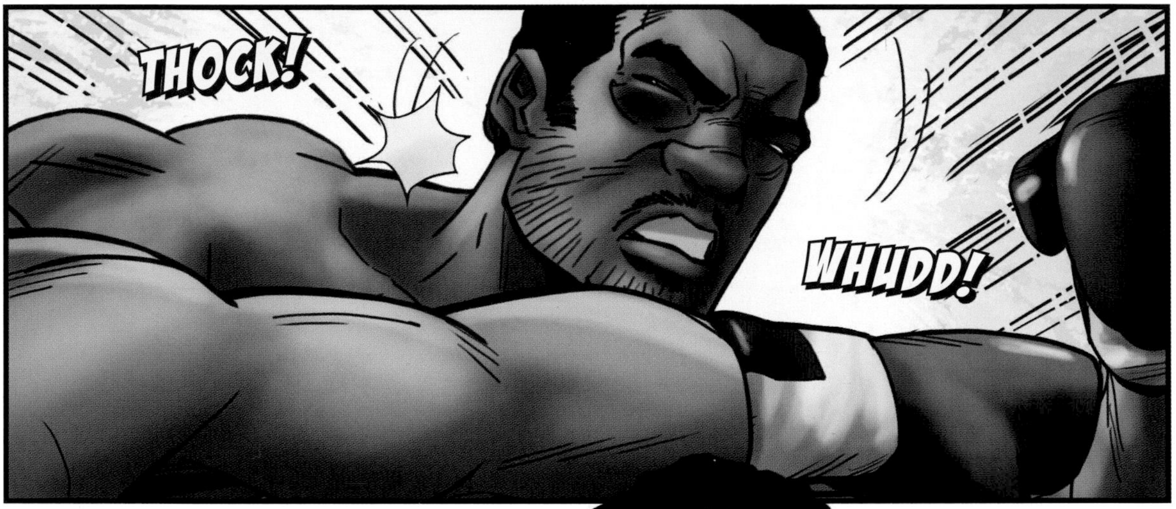
THOCK!
WHUDD!

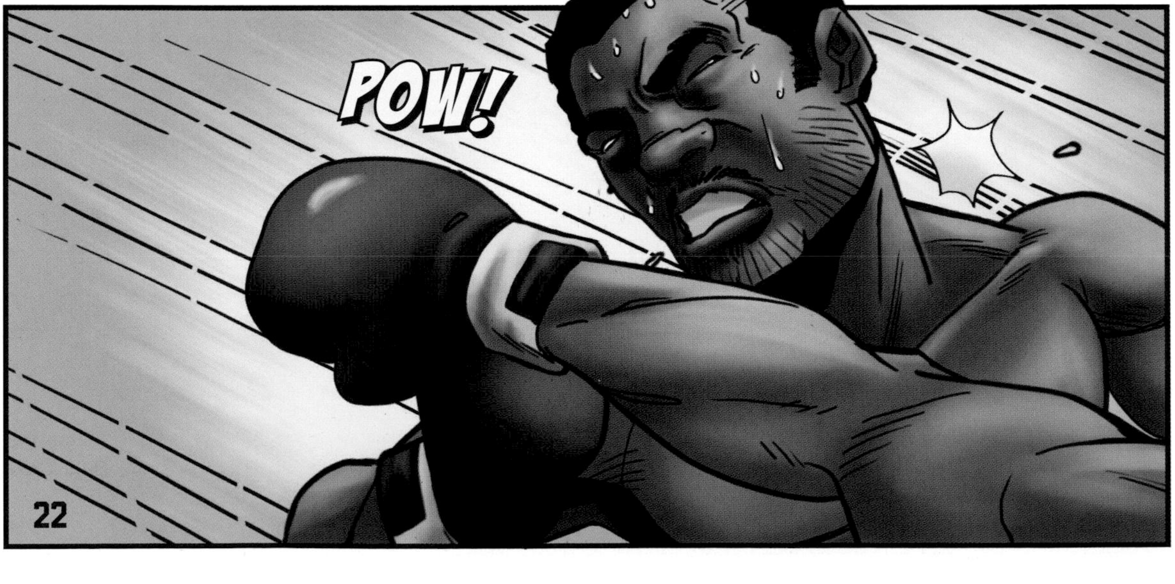
POW!

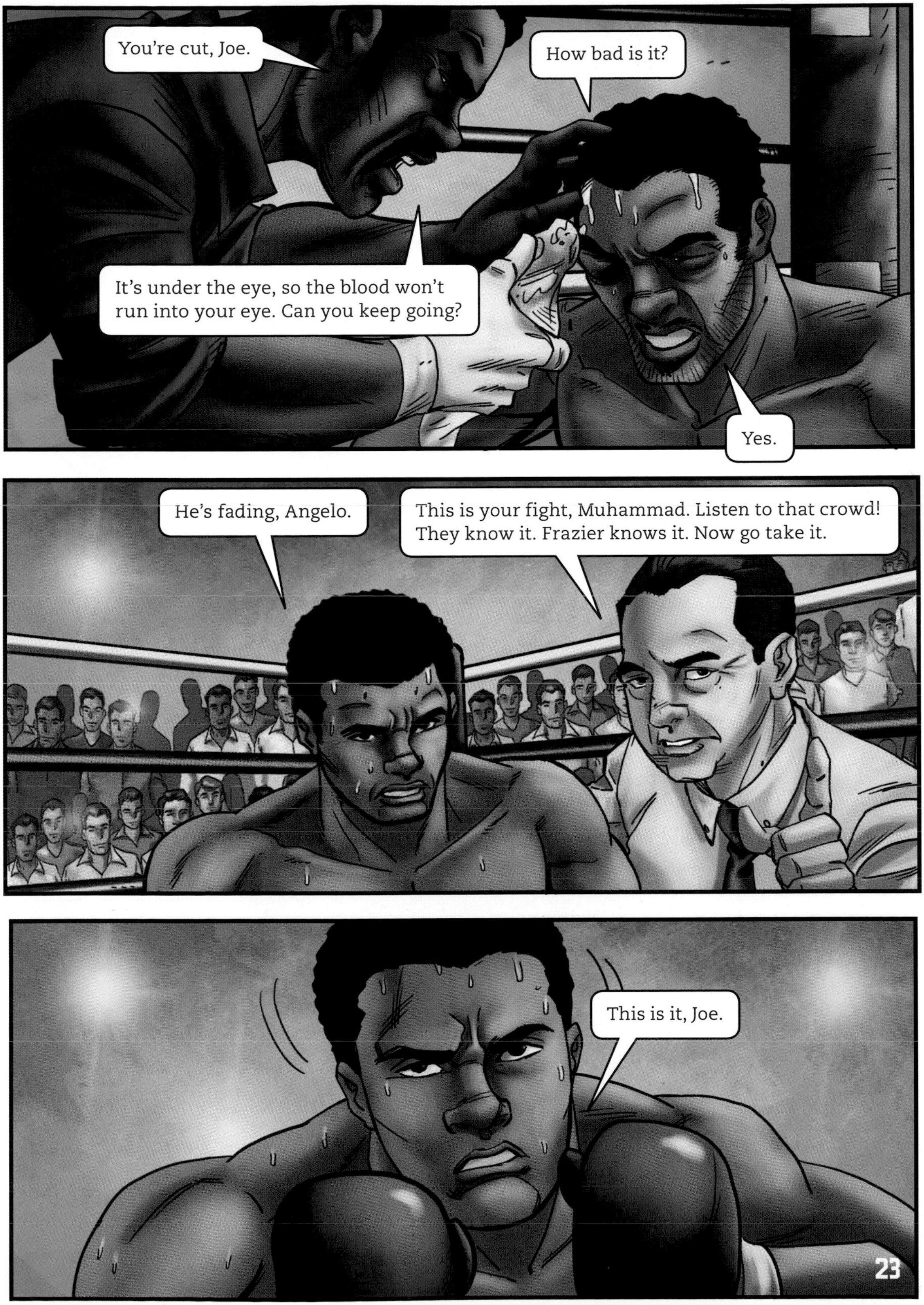
You're cut, Joe.
How bad is it?
It's under the eye, so the blood won't run into your eye. Can you keep going?
Yes.
He's fading, Angelo.
This is your fight, Muhammad. Listen to that crowd! They know it. Frazier knows it. Now go take it.
This is it, Joe.

THE FINAL BELL

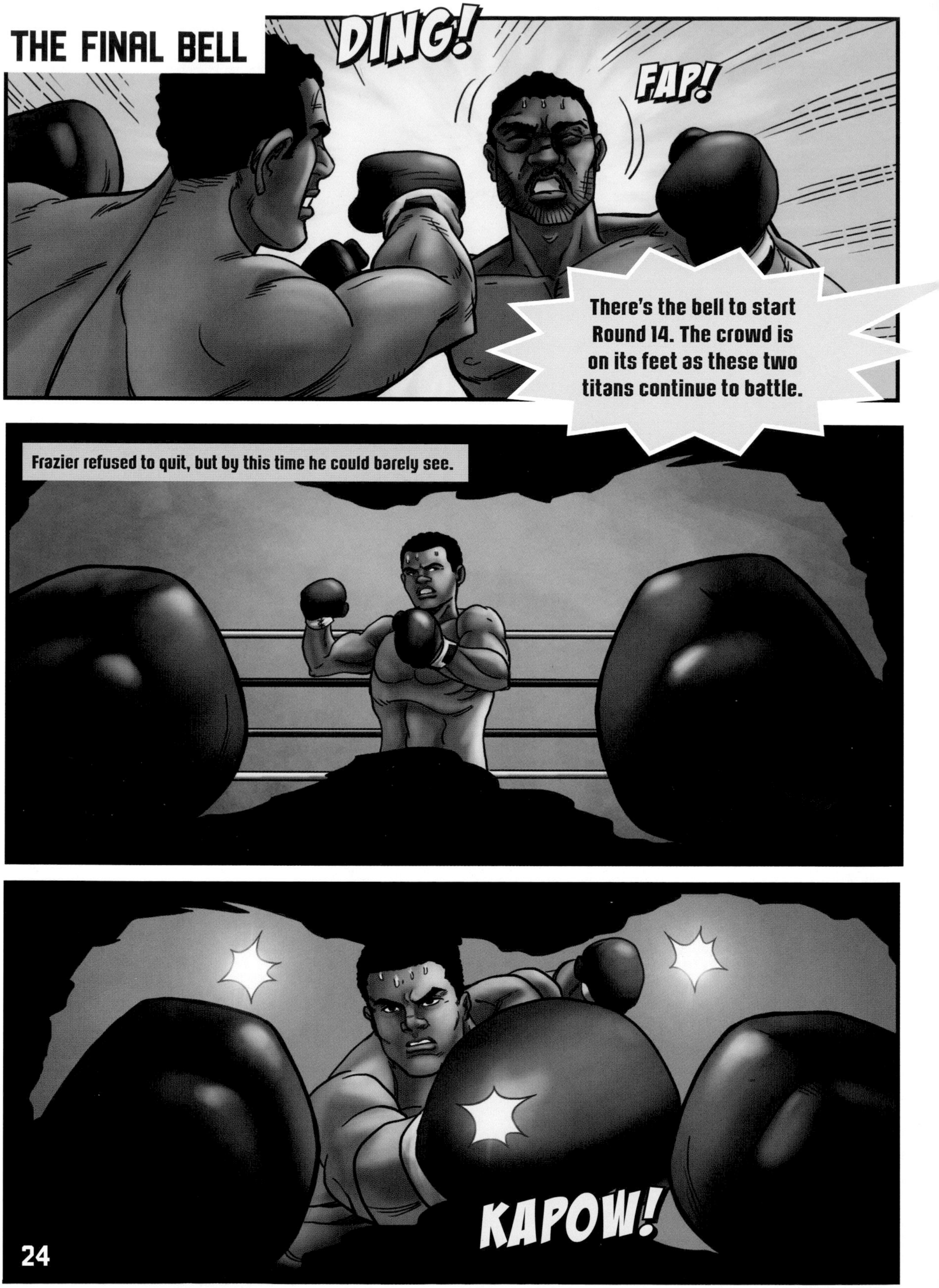
DING!
FAP!
There's the bell to start Round 14. The crowd is on its feet as these two titans continue to battle.
Frazier refused to quit, but by this time he could barely see.
KAPOW!

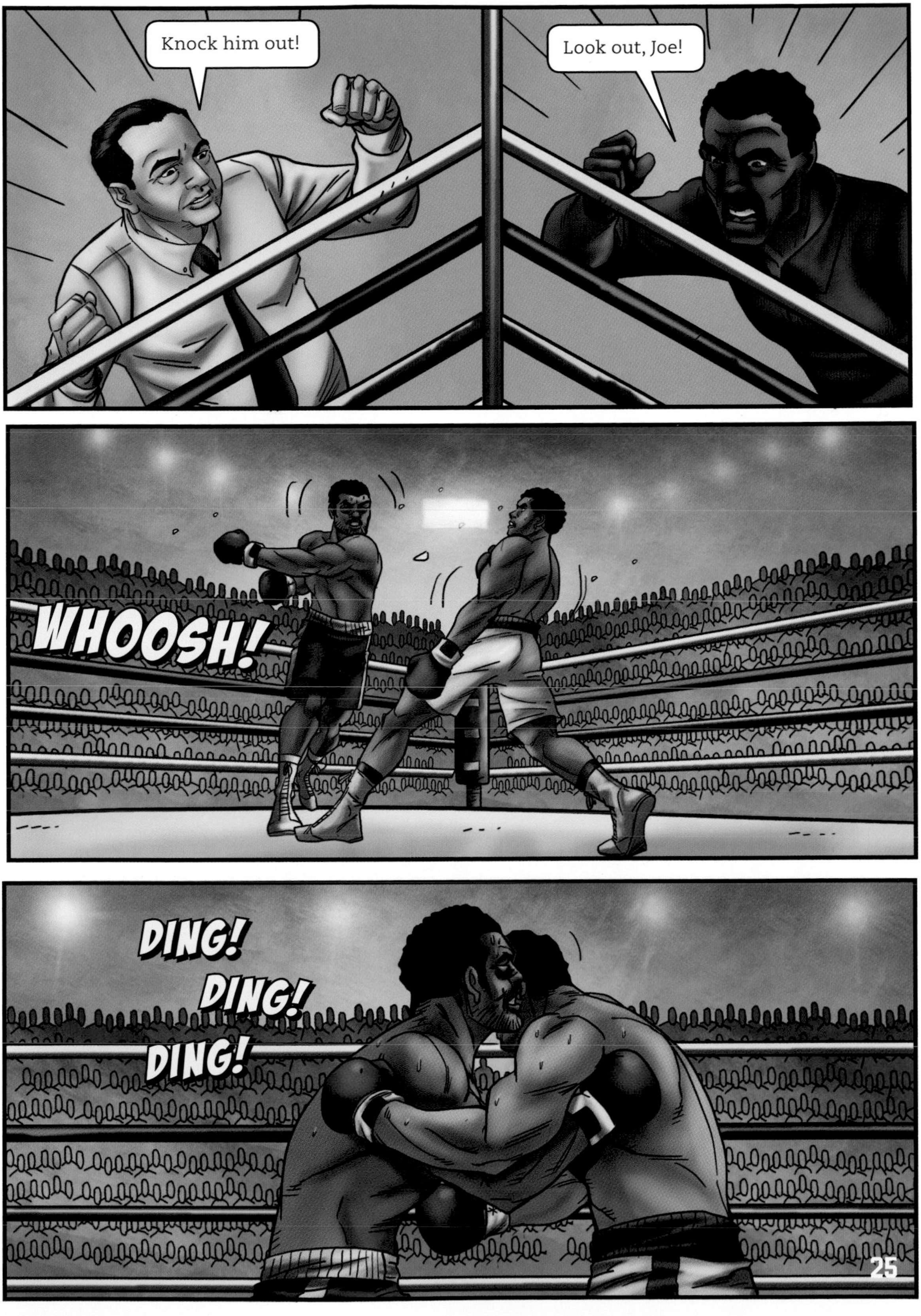
Knock him out!
Look out, Joe!
WHOOSH!
DING!
DING!
DING!

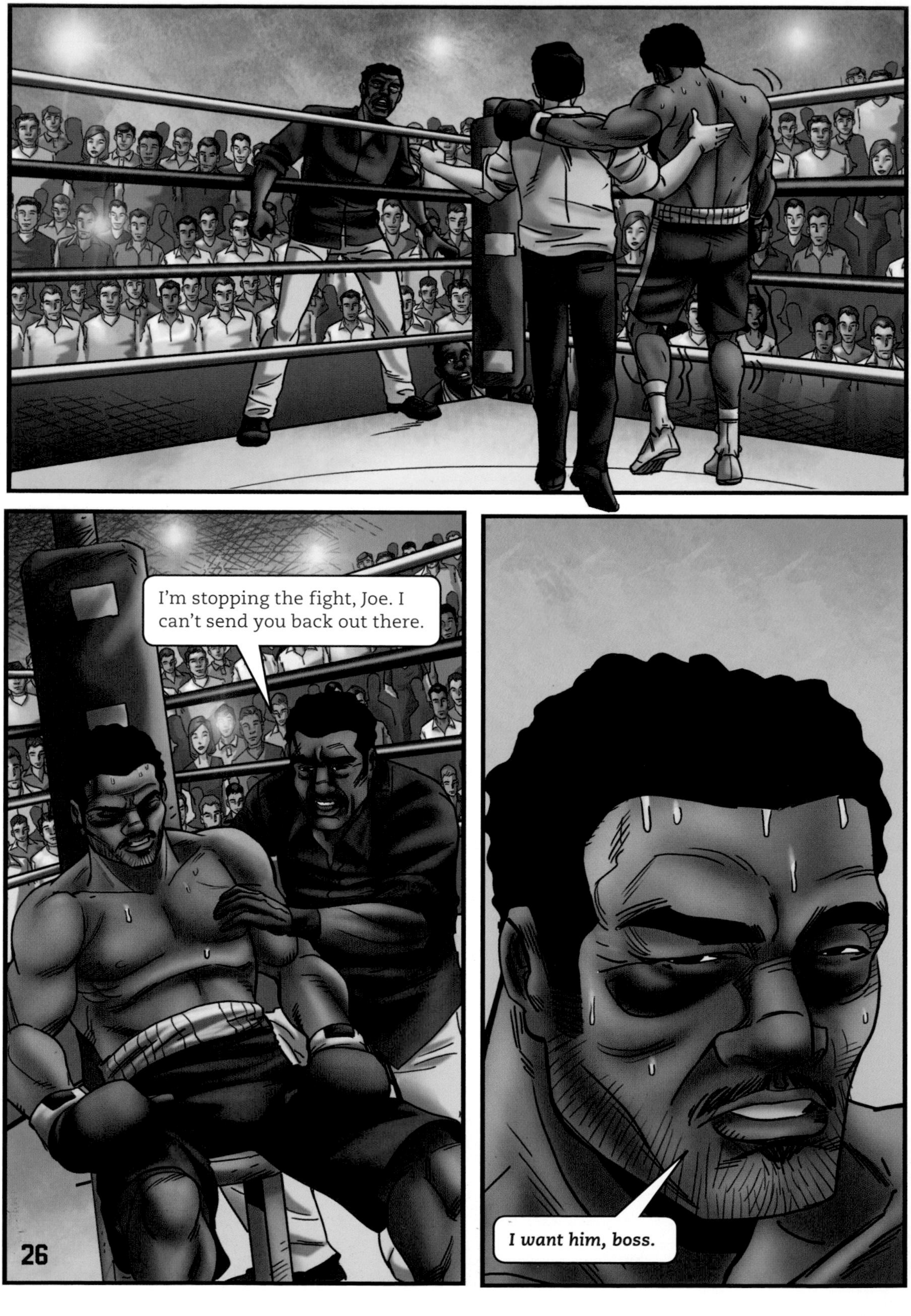
I'm stopping the fight, Joe. I can't send you back out there.
I want him, boss.

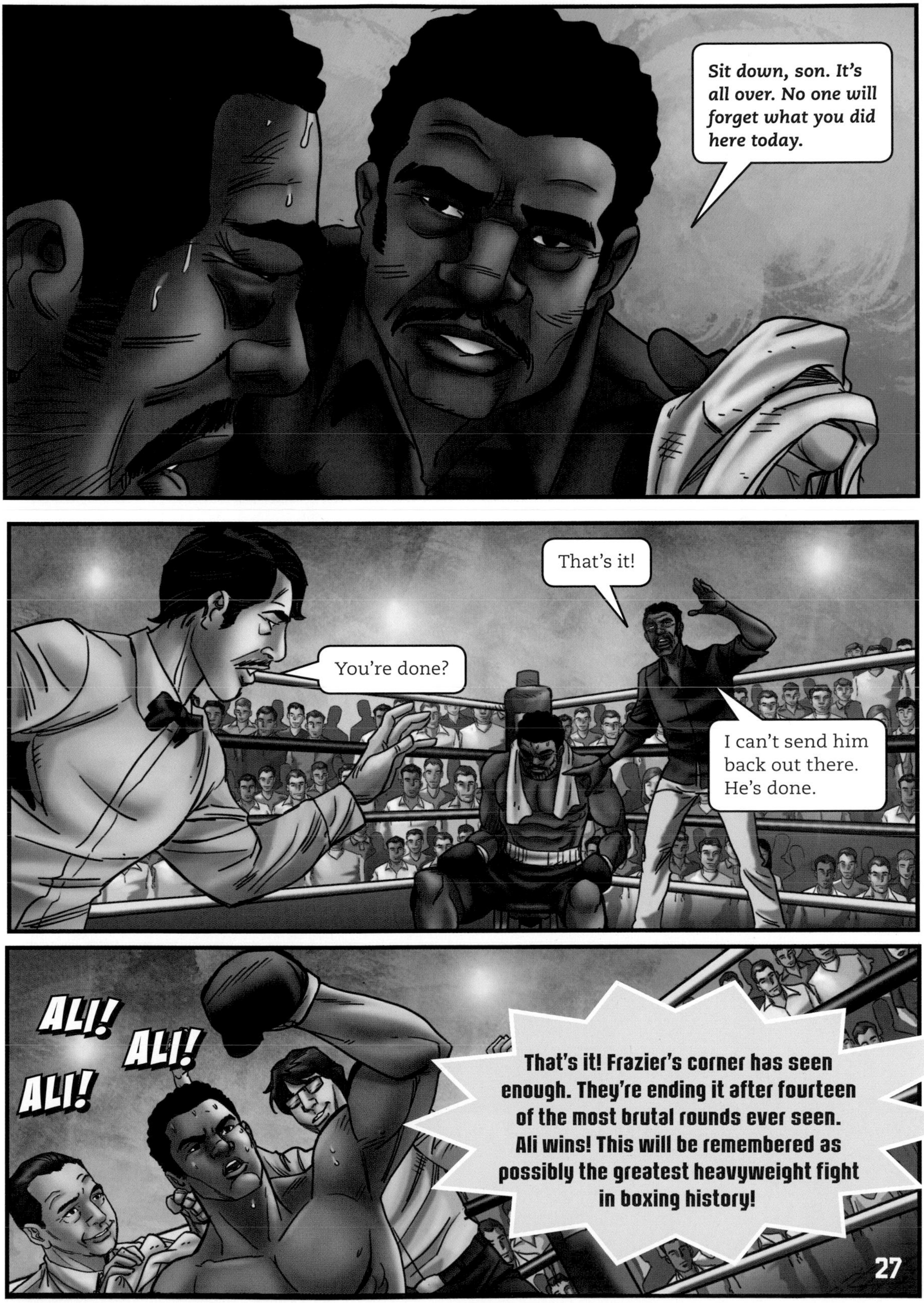
Sit down, son. It's all over. No one will forget what you did here today.
You're done?
That's it!
I can't send him back out there. He's done.
ALI!
ALI!
ALI!
That's it! Frazier's corner has seen enough. They're ending it after fourteen of the most brutal rounds ever seen. Ali wins! This will be remembered as possibly the greatest heavyweight fight in boxing history!

RIVALS TO THE END

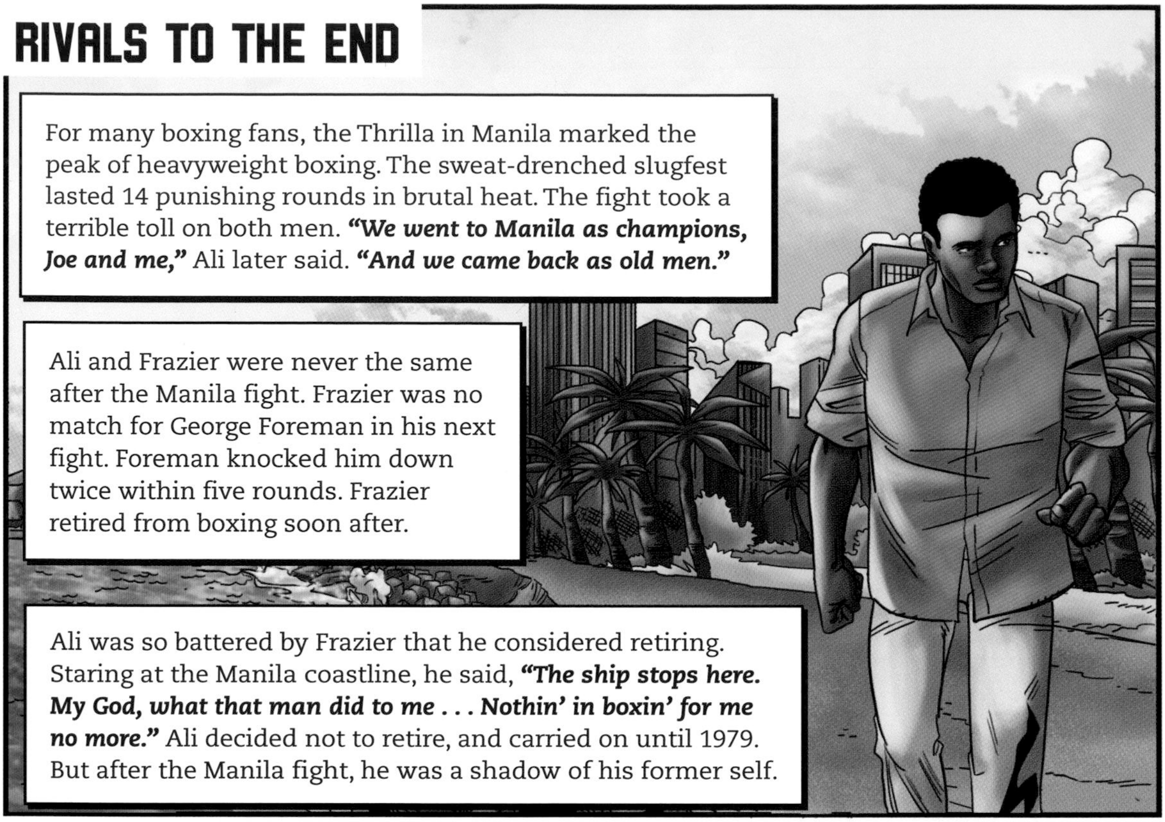
For many boxing fans, the Thrilla in Manila marked the peak of heavyweight boxing. The sweat-drenched slugfest lasted 14 punishing rounds in brutal heat. The fight took a terrible toll on both men. ***"We went to Manila as champions, Joe and me,"*** Ali later said. ***"And we came back as old men."***
Ali and Frazier were never the same after the Manila fight. Frazier was no match for George Foreman in his next fight. Foreman knocked him down twice within five rounds. Frazier retired from boxing soon after.
Ali was so battered by Frazier that he considered retiring. Staring at the Manila coastline, he said, ***"The ship stops here. My God, what that man did to me . . . Nothin' in boxin' for me no more."*** Ali decided not to retire, and carried on until 1979. But after the Manila fight, he was a shadow of his former self.

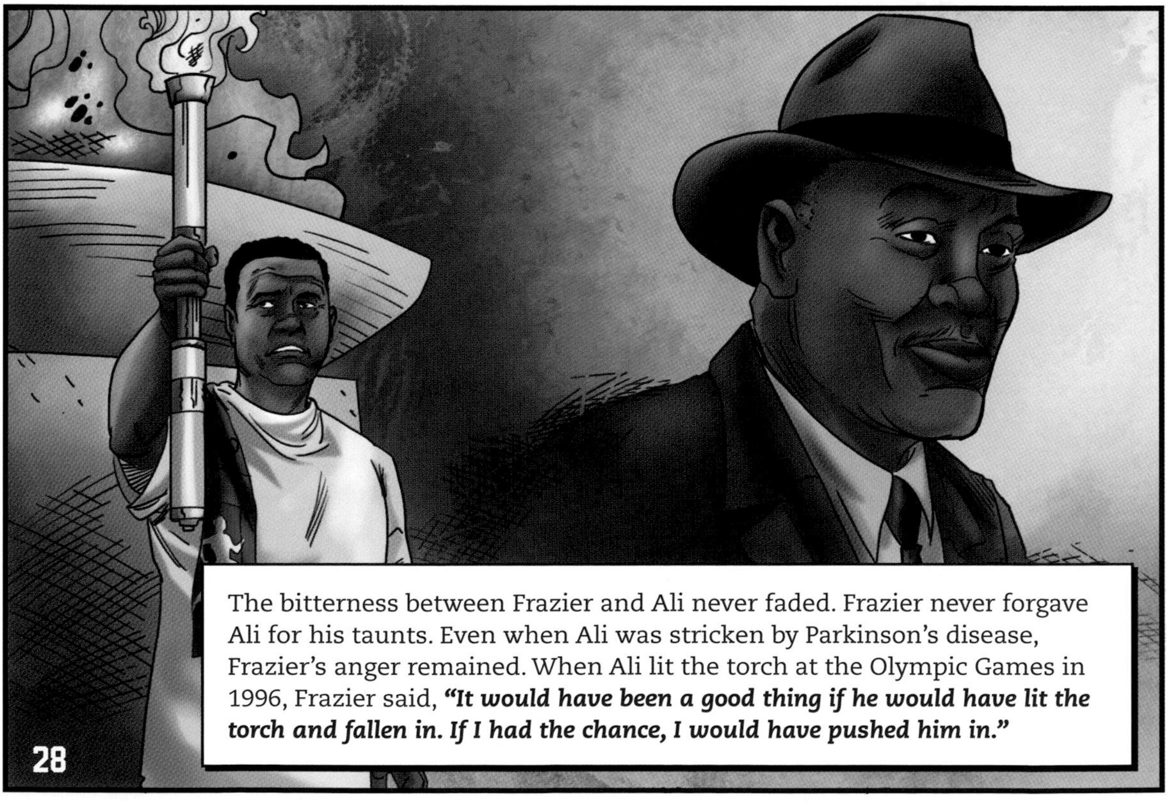
The bitterness between Frazier and Ali never faded. Frazier never forgave Ali for his taunts. Even when Ali was stricken by Parkinson's disease, Frazier's anger remained. When Ali lit the torch at the Olympic Games in 1996, Frazier said, ***"It would have been a good thing if he would have lit the torch and fallen in. If I had the chance, I would have pushed him in."***

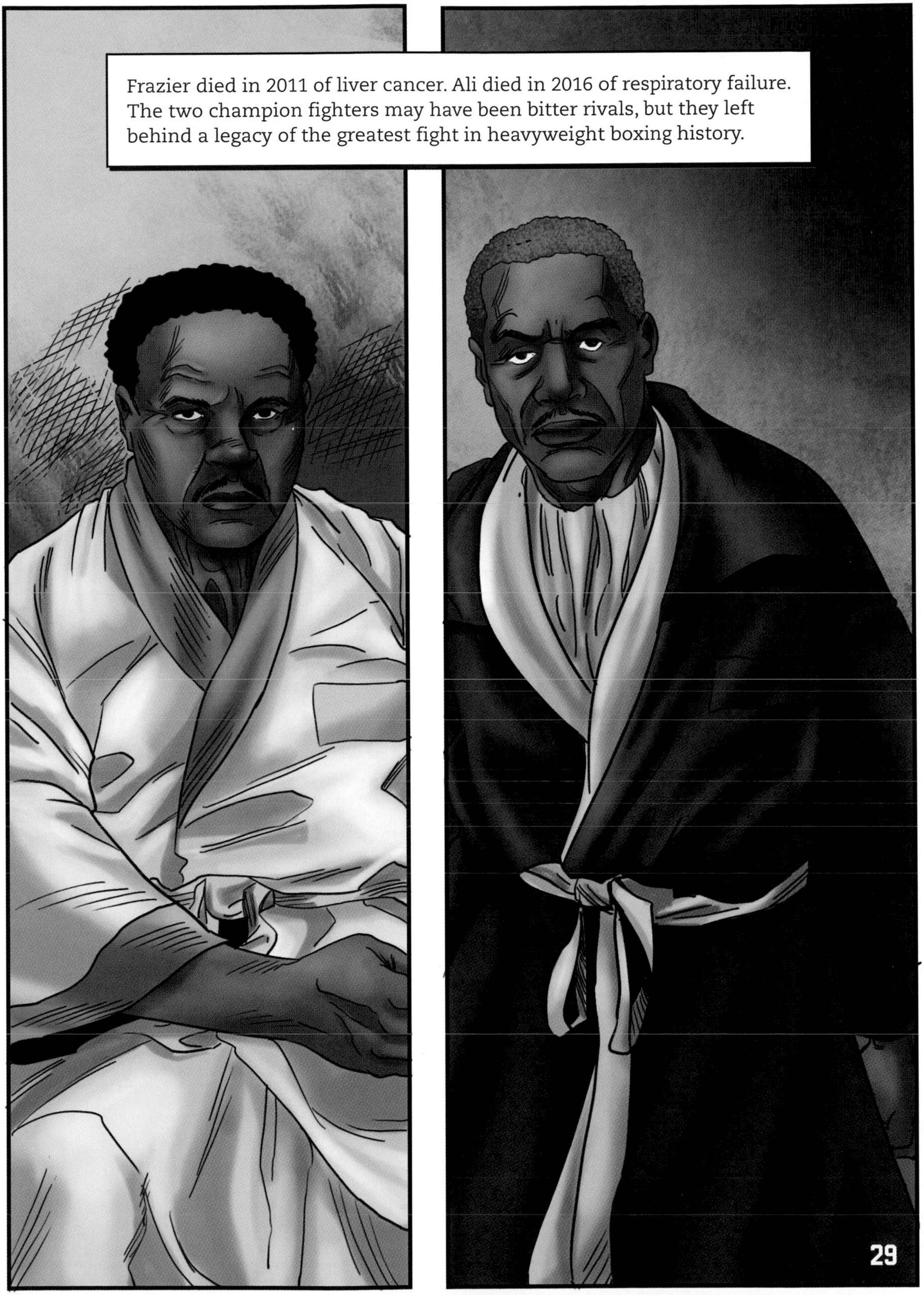
Frazier died in 2011 of liver cancer. Ali died in 2016 of respiratory failure. The two champion fighters may have been bitter rivals, but they left behind a legacy of the greatest fight in heavyweight boxing history.

GLOSSARY

jab (JAB)—a short, straight punch

promoter (pruh-MOH-tur)—a person or company that sets up and publicizes a sporting event

retire (rih-TIRE)—to end one's career

rival (RYE-vuhl)—an opponent with whom one has an ongoing competition

rope-a-dope (ROPE-uh-dope)—a strategy in which a boxer leans on the ropes and protects his head while allowing an opponent to punch him repeatedly; the goal is to let the opponent tire himself out while not taking serious damage

strategy (STRAT-uh-jee)—a plan to achieve a goal or win a competition

upper cut (UP-ur CUT)—a swinging punch in which the arm travels upward to hit an opponent's chin

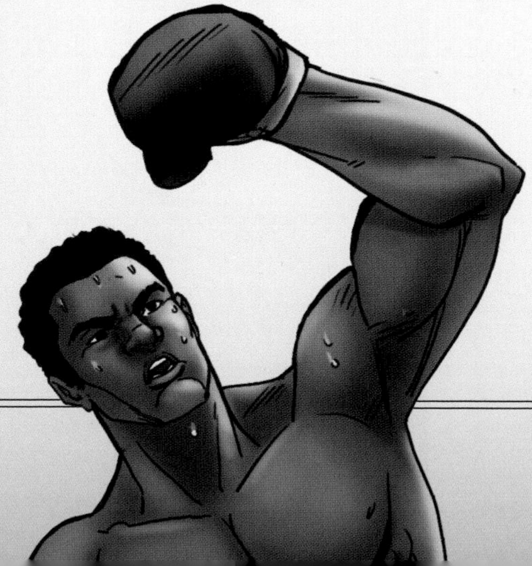

READ MORE

Burgan, Michael. *Ali's Knockout Punch: How a Photograph Stunned the Boxing World.* Captured History Sports. North Mankato, Minnesota: Compass Point Books, 2017.

Denenberg, Barry. *Ali: An American Champion.* New York: Simon & Schuster Books for Young Readers, 2014.

Doeden, Matt. *Muhammad Ali: The Greatest.* Gateway Biographies. Minneapolis: Lerner Publications, 2017.

CRITICAL THINKING QUESTIONS

- Muhammad Ali loved to taunt his opponents. Why do you think he did it?

- Frazier's corner threw in the towel with just one round remaining. Was it the right decision? Could Frazier have lasted another round?

- Frazier never forgave Ali for his taunts. Put yourself in Frazier's place. Could you have forgiven Ali? Why or why not?

INTERNET SITES

Use Facthound to find Internet sites related to this book.

Visit *www.facthound.com*

Just type in 9781543528664 and go.

Check out projects, games and lots more at
www.capstonekids.com

INDEX